U.S.-China Economic and Security Review Commission Staff Report

January 2011
(information current as of November 2010)

THE NATIONAL SECURITY IMPLICATIONS OF INVESTMENTS AND PRODUCTS FROM THE PEOPLE'S REPUBLIC OF CHINA IN THE TELECOMMUNICATIONS SECTOR

by USCC Research Staff

supported by Reperi LLC

1

NOTICE

This paper presents an open source analysis of the impact on U.S. national security interests of China's extensive engagement in the U.S. telecommunications sector.

The paper's research covers the following:
- The nature of changes in the U.S. telecommunications supply chains and the impacts on U.S. national security.
- The technological trends in telecommunications and related technologies.
- The People's Republic of China's (PRC) direct and indirect investment trends in telecommunications and related technologies and in the U.S. telecommunications marketplace.
- The nature of the People's Republic of China's direct and indirect ownership, control, and influence in the U.S. telecommunications supply chain.
- The penetration of the U.S. marketplace by companies subject to ownership, control, or influence by the People's Republic of China.
- The locations where products designed, engineered, or manufactured in China or supplied by companies subject to control or influence by China may appear in the U.S. marketplace and critical supply chains.
- The trends in the marketplace that can be attributed to the influence of China's ubiquitous presence in U.S. supply chains.
- The nature of relationship-building between U.S. companies and companies located in and/or subject to control or influence by the People's Republic of China.
- The potential vulnerabilities of critical elements of the U.S. telecommunications market exploitable by actors in supply chain segments.
- The assessment of potential cyber security impacts.
- The means of assessing telecommunications and supply chain vulnerabilities.
- The impacts of present and emerging vulnerabilities on U.S. defense contractors and government procurement functions.

TABLE OF CONTENTS

INTRODUCTION

The increased presence of Chinese telecommunications products and services in the American marketplace is the result of bilateral investment between the United States and China. Chinese companies have offered U.S. investors (investment banks, venture firms, business investors, and others) opportunities to balance risk and gain potentially higher rates of return by participating in the world's fastest-growing emerging market. By outsourcing some aspects of operations, U.S. businesses and multinational corporations have been able to increase the amount of value built into products compared to the same dollars expended domestically and have further been able to diversify market holdings in Asia after reaching saturation points in U.S. and European markets.

In a similar way, Chinese companies are increasingly looking to the American market to open up new opportunities.[1] U.S. companies have offered Chinese firms and investment funds access to established business models and advanced research and development processes, increased efficiencies in select areas of business, and opportunities in the world's wealthiest market. Aside from raising their own levels of technical and management expertise, they are also able to affiliate their products with the excellent reputation of U.S. brands in global markets. China's technology industry now appears to be a de facto part of the American communications industry landscape. Based on current market realities, the presence and continued growth of products with at least partial manufacturing and development origins in China will continue to increase and pervade most areas of American life, business, and government.

Chinese telecommunications companies are also actively expanding into global markets. In emerging markets not encumbered by existing legacy infrastructures, demand for new telecom capabilities is often best met by utilizing generation-leaping technologies, a phenomenon that is helping to drive a large global appetite for leading-edge technological innovation. Chinese telecom technology companies are aggressively pursuing customers in emerging communications technologies – and are thus gaining traction in global markets, particularly emerging markets.

The expansion strategy of Chinese telecoms is becoming increasingly more effective as business acumen gained from joint ventures, partnerships, and acquisitions improves their competitive capabilities. Chinese companies have also thoughtfully cultivated global management and recruitment models that are helping them move into positions of global leadership through management excellence.[2] Direct and indirect investment from developed countries into Chinese telecom and technology ventures, and China's own strategic acquisitions of technological know-how and physical infrastructures in other emerging markets, are also facilitating their emergence as a formidable global competitor.

Many aspects of the future global telecom and technology markets are now being shaped by Chinese business and governmental interests. The momentum they are gaining and the way they are applying their advantages are transforming global markets, propelling Chinese telecom

---

[1] Dezan Shira & Associates, "Made in USA: China and India Invest Abroad," May 13, 2010. _http://www.2point6billion.com/news/2010/05/13/made-in-usa-china-and-india-invest-abroad-5645.html._
[2] Northrop Grumman Corporation, "Capability of the People's Republic of China to Conduct Cyber Warfare and Computer Network Exploitation" (contracted research paper for the U.S.-China Economic and Security ReviewCommission, June 2009). _http://www.uscc.gov/researchpapers/2009/NorthropGrumman_PRC_Cyber_Paper_FINAL_Approved%20Report_16 Oct2009.pdf._

and technology ventures toward the leading edge of technology development, manufacturing, and standards setting. If current trends continue, China (combined with proxy interests) will effectively become the principal market driver in many sectors, including telecom, on the basis of consumption, production, and innovation.

This greater potential role for China has generated concerns regarding corresponding potential national security implications of manufacturing and investment by China's telecommunications companies. Signals intelligence (SIGINT) is a significant source of Chinese intelligence collection,[3] and there is growing public concern over the impacts of cyber espionage incidents that appear to originate in China.[4] Furthermore, large China-based, -owned, or -influenced companies – particularly those "national champions" prominent in China's "going out" strategy of overseas expansion – are subject to government direction, to include support for PRC (People's Republic of China) state policies and political goals.[5] In light of this, the large footprints of Chinese state-affiliated companies in global telecommunications markets, and their acquisitions in part or in whole of western telecom firms, may generate concerns in some quarters that this may facilitate increased intelligence exploitation of international communications and computer networks by Chinese state-affiliated entities. Concern over growing Chinese influence in this arena is not unfounded, but should be balanced by a realistic assessment of communications security vulnerabilities as well as by an appreciation of the symbiosis that has developed between the Chinese and western telecommunications industries.

The greatest potential impact on the United States could come in the form of Chinese investments in U.S. telecommunications companies. The vast global telecommunications and technology infrastructures owned or operated by these companies include undersea, terrestrial, wireless, and space-based networks. These investments would increase China's leverage in the U.S. marketplace and beyond (even if indirectly through joint ventures and third parties) and could eventually provide China access to or control of vital U.S. and allied information, networks, or segments of critical supply chains.

Another key concern regarding the security of U.S. communication and computer networks relates to the reliability of electronics components found within the network hardware. National security vulnerabilities attributable to having critical infrastructure components manufactured, implemented, operated, or maintained by foreign actors are increasing at an escalated rate. Within government, steps can be taken to safeguard sensitive areas but at a substantially increased cost in both resources and lost opportunities to innovate. Trusted hardware and software produced domestically may cost more than commoditized products produced abroad. The government may also find that it will have to curb the infusion of ever-newer communications technologies into some especially sensitive areas in favor of retaining secure legacy technology models.

---

[3] Interagency OPSEC (Operations Security) Support Staff, *Intelligence Threat Handbook* (June 2004), p. 23. *http://www.fas.org/irp/threat/handbook/foreign.pdf* ; and Interagency OPSEC Support Staff, *Intelligence Threat Handbook – Selected Supplemental Intelligence Service Information* (June 2004), pp. 75-76. *http://www.fas.org/irp/threat/handbook/supplement.pdf*.

[4] Northrop Grumman Corporation, "Capability of the People's Republic of China to Conduct Cyber Warfare and Computer Network Exploitation" (contracted research paper for the U.S.-China Economic and Security Review Commission, June 2009). *http://www.uscc.gov/researchpapers/2009/NorthropGrumman_PRC_Cyber_Paper_FINAL_Approved%20Report_16 Oct2009.pdf*

[5] For a detailed explanation and examples of this phenomenon, see "China, Inc.: The Party and Business," chapter 2, in Richard McGregor, *The Party: The Secret World of China's Communist Rulers* (New York: Harper Collins, 2010).

Staking out a middle course between being unduly alarmist and unduly complacent, this report seeks to lay out in greater detail many of the issues involved in the international investments made by Chinese telecommunications firms. It also seeks to describe some of the *potential* security vulnerabilities in communications networks that might be exploited by hostile actors, whether state sponsored or otherwise. It is hoped that this will help to better illuminate for Congress and the general public a critical area of concern that stands astride the crossroads of U.S. national security and future economic security.

SECTION 1
MACRO-LEVEL PATTERNS OF CHINA'S
TELECOM INVESTMENT ACTIVITIES

The Chinese government treats the telecommunications sector as a "strategic" industry *(see text box below)* and has expended significant effort and resources to promote and enable new business opportunities in the telecommunications field. These efforts are supported by national-level policies, as the country's senior leadership perceives investment in high-technology sectors to be instrumental in closing the technological gap between China and western nations.[6] The large and growing state-controlled telecommunications sector is also a major source of government revenue. As stated by political scientist Cheng Li:

> *The Chinese government has always considered the telecom sector to be one of the most strategically important and commercially lucrative industries in the country. [As of] 2005, the six leading Chinese telecom operation providers [were]: China Telecom, China Mobile, China Netcom, China Unicom, China Railcom, and China Satcom, all of which [were] state-owned enterprises (SOEs), reported that they had total assets of 10.6 trillion yuan, revenues of 6.6 trillion yuan, and profits of 600 billion yuan. [As of that year,] [t]hese six companies constituted one-sixth of the total assets, and 20 percent of the profits, of all of the enterprises directly under the leadership of the State-Owned Assets Supervision and Administration Commission.[7]*

National security concerns have accompanied the dramatic growth of China's telecom sector. Signals intelligence is a significant source of Chinese intelligence collection,[8] and there is growing public concern over the impacts of cyber espionage incidents that appear to originate in China.[9] Additionally, large Chinese companies – particularly those "national champions" prominent in China's "going out" strategy[10] of overseas expansion – are directly subject to direction by the Chinese Communist Party (CCP), to include support for PRC state policies and goals.[11] From this point of view, the clear economic benefits of foreign investment in the United States must be weighed against the *potential* security concerns related to infrastructure

---

[6] Evan Feigenbaum, *China's Techno-Warriors: National Security and Strategic Competition from the Nuclear to the Information Age* (Palo Alto, CA: Stanford University Press, 2003).

[7] Cheng Li, "China's Telecom Industry on the Move: Domestic Competition, Global Ambition, and Leadership Transition," *China Leadership Monitor* 19 (2006).

[8] Interagency OPSEC Support Staff, *Intelligence Threat Handbook* (June 2004), p. 23. http://www.fas.org/irp/threat/handbook/foreign.pdf ; and Interagency OPSEC Support Staff, *Intelligence Threat Handbook – Selected Supplemental Intelligence Service Information* (June 2004), pp. 75-76. http://www.fas.org/irp/threat/handbook/supplement.pdf .

[9] Northrop Grumman Corporation, "Capability of the People's Republic of China to Conduct Cyber Warfare and Computer Network Exploitation" (contracted research paper for the U.S.-China Economic and Security Review Commission, June 2009). http://www.uscc.gov/researchpapers/2009/NorthropGrumman_PRC_Cyber_Paper_FINAL_Approved%20Report_16 Oct2009.pdf

[10] The "Going Out" strategy is a Chinese government campaign introduced at the 2002 Communist Party Congress to raise China's global economic profile by investing overseas and acquiring foreign assets. See U.S.-China Economic and Security Review Commission, *Annual Report to Congress 2009* (Washington, DC: U.S. Government Printing Office, November 2009), p. 94, footnote #52. See also Jamil Anderlini, "China to Deploy Forex Reserves," *Financial Times*, July 21, 2009; and Accenture Consulting, "China Spreads Its Wings: Chinese Companies Go Global," 2007.

[11] For a detailed explanation and examples of this phenomenon, see "China, Inc.: The Party and Business," chapter 2, in Richard McGregor, *The Party: The Secret World of China's Communist Rulers* (New York: Harper Collins, 2010).

components coming under the control of foreign entities. This seems particularly applicable in the telecommunications industry, as Chinese companies continue systematically to acquire significant holdings in prominent global and U.S. telecommunications and information technology companies.[12]

Some analysts also believe that the government of the People's Republic of China is interested in acquiring meaningful stakes in companies that have significant influence in other national governments. This particularly applies to companies that also have significant investment or stakes in China's markets (such as technology and telecommunications equipment providers). Influencing the behavior of multinational companies with this form of leverage may be one logical way for the Chinese government to seek to protect its interests in a global context.[13]

Telecommunications as a "Strategic" Industry in China

Telecommunications is one of seven "strategic industries" in which the Chinese government seeks to maintain "absolute control" (meaning over 50 percent ownership). The government also wishes to maintain a dominant presence in six "heavyweight" industries through regulation and government control. These industries are as follows:[14]

Strategic Industries:	Heavyweight Industries:
(1) Armaments	(1) Machinery
(2) Power Generation and Distribution	(2) Automobiles
(3) Oil and Petrochemicals	(3) Information Technology
(4) Telecommunications	(4) Construction
(5) Coal	(5) Iron and Steel
(6) Civil Aviation	(6) Nonferrous Metals
(7) Shipping	

The Chinese government has actively sought to cultivate state-controlled "national champions" companies in these sectors.[15] It has also offered state support to companies in its "strategic" and "heavyweight" industries, such as land and energy subsidies, favorable tax policies, and below-market interest rate loans issued from state banks with reduced or no expectation of repayment.[16] The PRC's "national champions" are a centerpiece of the government's "going out" strategy to cultivate state-controlled firms capable of competing in the international marketplace.[17]

---

[12] For examples of overseas acquisitions made, or sought, in 2010 by Chinese telecommunications companies, see (1) A pending purchase of Nigerian Telecom (Nitel) by China Unicom, in "Rumor: China Unicom Leads Nitel Acquisition," C114.com, October 16, 2010. *http://www.cn-c114.net/583/a550716.html*; and (2) the statement that China Telecom "will 'closely examine' opportunities for overseas acquisitions" as it moves into markets such as that of India, in Peter Stein and Yun-Hee Kim, "China Firm Eyes India," *Wall Street Journal,* September 28, 2010.

[13] Wayne M. Morrison and Marc Labonte, "China's Holdings of U.S. Securities: Implications for the U.S. Economy," (Washington, DC: Congressional Research Service, CRS-7, January 9, 2008).

[14] U.S.-China Economic and Security Review Commission, *Annual Report to Congress 2009* (Washington, DC: U.S. Government Printing Office, November 2009), p. 59. For the underlying source, see U.S.-China Economic and Security Review Commission, *Hearing on the Extent of the Government's Control of China's Economy, and Implications for the United States*, written testimony of Barry Naughton and George Haley, May 24, 2007.

[15] U.S.-China Economic and Security Review Commission, *Hearing on the Extent of the Government's Control of China's Economy, and Implications for the United States*, written testimony of Barry Naughton , May 24, 2007.

[16] U.S.-China Economic and Security Review Commission, *Annual Report to Congress 2009* (Washington, DC: U.S. Govrnment Printing Office, November 2009), pp. 57-65.

[17] Accenture Consulting, "China Spreads Its Wings: Chinese Companies Go Global," 2007. *http://www.accenture.com/NR/rdonlyres/1F79806F-E076-4CD7-8B74-3BAFBAC58943/0/6341_chn_spreads_wings_final8.pdf*

Some large Chinese companies, such as the telecommunications firm Huawei and the computer manufacturer Lenovo, retain a "hybrid" structure as "national champions" that receive favorable treatment through close government ties while also enjoying the freedom to operate as private companies domestically and abroad without bearing the onus of government ties.[18] *(See more on the background of Huawei on pp. 13-18, of ZTE on pp. 21-23, and of Lenovo on pp. 66-68).*

Global Telecommunications Market Trends in 2008-2009

The merger and acquisition (M&A) environment in the telecommunications industry is active, and there are fast-growing markets worldwide, particularly in the developing world, Europe, and the United States.[19] More deals between U.S. and Chinese entities are likely to appear in the future: China has money to spend, telecommunications is a core strategic industry of interest, and a huge percentage of telecom equipment is manufactured in China. Therefore, it is reasonable to expect to see a global presence for Chinese companies as an acquirer and consolidator of assets and as a developer of new market opportunities.

Due to the global nature of communications and information markets, business trends in telecommunications are very often going to flow in a global context, with business transactions occurring within national contexts representing subtrends that will still seek centers of gravity created by global trends. M&A activity in telecommunications tends to fall into two categories:

A. Consolidations within mature markets.
B. Growth opportunities in emerging markets.

Some telecommunications businesses willing to risk emerging market hazards may wait for an emerging market's conditions to conform to favorable metrics before attempting to develop a telecom prospect. Early infrastructure developers/service providers may at times wait for opportunities that will allow them to time early risks and will have few intentions of remaining in that particular developing market long term. Their business objectives may be to remain in an emerging market only long enough to develop service areas sufficiently for them to be attractive M&A targets by more long-term-oriented operators.

Following the panic in financial markets in 2008-2009, large telecommunications industry players have been waiting for greater economic distress to push M&A costs down to bargain-basement prices, but this did not happen as fully as had been anticipated. The year 2009 was characterized by "prospecting" in the telecom industry. Few actual mergers & acquisitions deals occurred, however, as deeply discounted bargains did not materialize as much as might have been expected or hoped for by prospective buyers. Future trends are likely to see a continual and marked increase in bids and sales as prospective buyers come back to bargaining tables with more realistic expectations.[20]

Lingering economic distress will undoubtedly push some vulnerable firms past the tipping point; therefore, the future telecom marketplace, both globally and in the United States, should see

---

[18] Geoff Dyer and Richard McGregor, "China's Champions: Why State Ownership Is No Longer a Dead Hand," *Financial Times*, March 16, 2008.

[19] Within the United States, a great deal of new focus is to be found in rural markets, in particular.

[20] "Up to Bat Again – Will it be Strike Two for Huawei in the U.S.?" Bill Newman Inbound Acquisitions and Investments Blog, quoting *Financial Times* article, April 16, 2010.

many M&A deals. Globally, telecom businesses are becoming much more tough-minded, are holding their most profitable business units back from M&A's as they are best able to do so, and are disposing of underperforming business units much faster than might have been the case in the past.

CHINESE TELECOM COMPANIES ENTER THE U.S. MARKET

China: Developer and Provider within China, and Global Exporter of Wireless and Next Generation Networks

As wireless networking comes under cost pressures in the United States, more incentive has been created in the U.S. market to consider alternative vendors. By keeping costs down and moving ahead to next generation technologies, Chinese manufacturers have taken much of the initiative in developing the Worldwide Interoperability for Microwave Access (WiMAX)[21] and LTE (Long-Term Evolution) standards. As one example of ways in which these companies are creating more opportunities for themselves through innovation and partnerships, press reports have indicated that Huawei will provide equipment to Leap Wireless (Cricket) to support their wireless initiatives.[22]

Meanwhile, the United States has been slower to respond to demands for newer technology standards. U.S. wireless providers are under enormous cost pressures while also being subject to increasing regulatory pressures to open their networks and create network and device interoperability. This comes on the heels of paying off expensive spectrum auctions purchased in efforts to create more contiguous networks.[23] The U.S. market has also been more difficult to penetrate due to security and regulatory concerns, such as those raised by the Committee on Foreign Investment in the United States when Huawei attempted to buy equipment manufacturer 3Com in 2008.[24] *(For more on these issues, see pp. 28-30.)*

China is poised to become the world's number one end-to-end supplier of telecom, cable, and mobile wireless equipment, much like AT&T and IBM dominated technology sectors in the past.[25] The global financial crisis pushed many telecom companies into severely vulnerable positions, allowing their market shares to be acquired easily by buyers as price competition increased globally. As wireless networking comes under cost pressures in the United States, more incentive has been created in the U.S. market to consider alternative vendors to remain competitive. Initially, many Chinese products were found only in certain parts of a telecom

---

[21] WiMAX (Worldwide Interoperability for Microwave Access), "What is WiMAX," WiMAX.com. *http://www.wimax.com/education*.
[22] "Huawei Supplies Leap Wireless," LightReading.com, August 15, 2006. *http://www.lightreading.com/document.asp?doc_id=101446.*
[23] A spectrum auction is "a process whereby a government uses an auction system to sell the rights to transmit signals over specific electromagnetic wavelengths." See "Spectrum Auction,"*Wikipedia.org. http://en.wikipedia.org/wiki/Spectrum_auction*. A major spectrum auction for the 700 megahertz frequency band, of interest to wireless providers, was held in January 2008. See Federal Communications Commission Press Release, "Auction of 700 MHz Band Licenses Scheduled for January 16, 2008 / Comment Sought on Competitive Bidding Procedures for Auction 73," August 17, 2007. *http://fjallfoss.fcc.gov/edocs_public/attachmatch/DA-07-3415A1.pdf*
[24] Bruce Einhorn, "Huawei's Business Deal Flops," *Business Week*, February 21, 2008.
[25] XChange Magazine, "Huawei: 'It' Vendor 2010," January 8, 2010, notes Huawei sales may be $36 billion in 2010 and take the place as the number one infrastructure supplier as it closes in on Ericsson. The world strength of global telecom deals by all Chinese firms, including ZTE, and scores of other companies may move China quickly to the number one slot across all categories.

network, but now Chinese companies rapidly are becoming the global, integral, "end-to-end" solution for telecom networks around the world.[26]

HUAWEI TECHNOLOGIES

Huawei Company Logo

Huawei Technologies [*Shenzhen Huawei Jishu Youxian Gongsi* / 深圳华为技术有限公司] is a high-technology enterprise that specializes in research and development (R&D), production, and marketing of communications equipment and providing customized network solutions for telecom carriers. Huawei has emerged as one of the largest global manufacturers of telecommunications equipment, particularly in the wireless market segment.

The dramatic growth of companies like Huawei is an extraordinary accomplishment.[27] By 2007, Huawei served 35 of the top 50 telecom operators and was investing 10 percent of revenue back into R&D each year.[28] By the end of 2009, Huawei was the world's second-largest telecom provider, ranking only behind the Swedish firm Ericsson.[29] The rise of Huawei has been so dramatic that some industry analysts have suspected "unsustainably low prices and government export assistance" as key to the company's rapid expansion.[30] *(See text box below.)* Others, however, would identify the key to the company's successes as its "sound business strategies," to include an early focus on underserviced markets in rural China, "to which multinational titans did not even bother to seek access."[31]

European Controversies over Alleged PRC State Support to Huawei

Allegations of PRC state subsidies to Huawei raised controversy in Europe in summer 2010, with both workers' unions and Option SA, a Belgian manufacturer of wireless wide-area network (WWAN) modems,[32] making complaints that Chinese government assistance to Huawei and ZTE allowed the Chinese companies to compete with an unfair pricing advantage.[33] According to Option SA's complaint, the companies received beneficial financing arrangements from PRC state banks, to include Huawei signing:

"…a cooperation agreement in September 2009 with the China Development Bank worth $30 billion—above its 2009 revenue of $22 billion and the sort of funding line the complaint said

---

[26] *China Technology and Telecom Sector M&A Report* 1st Quarter 2009, *www.cowenlatitude.com/document/09q1_china_tech_ma.pdf.*

[27] Annual Reports 2008, Cisco, Huawei, Motorola (Securities and Exchange Commission [SEC] 10K filings).

[28] "China's Technological Challenger", New *Zealand Herald*, March 15, 2007.

[29] Kevin O'Brien, "Upstart Chinese Telecom Company Rattles Industry as it Rises to No. 2", *New York Times,* November 29, 2009.

[30] "The Huawei Way", *Newsweek,* January 15, 2006.

[31] Cheng Li, "China's Telecom Industry on the Move: Domestic Competition, Global Ambition, and Leadership Transition", *China Leadership Monitor,* No. 19 (2006).

[32] Jonathan Stearns, "China Modem Makers May Face EU Anti-Subsidy Tariff," *Bloomberg,* September 16, 2010.

[33] Matthew Dalton, "Europe Raises Cry Over China Tech Exports," *Wall Street Journal,* October 5, 2010.

wouldn't be extended in a market economy... ZTE, with 2009 revenue of $8.4 billion, got a $15 billion credit line from the bank in March 2009. The complaint says these and other financing deals were provided with favorable terms, including three-year moratoriums on interest payments... Option said such terms have allowed Chinese companies to sell wireless modems in Europe for as little as €20 ($27) a device. Option would have to charge more than twice that much, it says, to earn a profit of 10% to 15% on its sales." [34]

In response to these complaints, in September 2010 the European Commission indicated that it would conduct an inquiry into whether Chinese-manufactured modems are "being subsidized and whether this subsidization has caused injury to the Union industry" and also ordered customs authorities to begin registering European Union (EU) imports of Chinese-manufactured WWAN modems as a preparatory action in the event that countervailing duties might be applied in the future. [35]

Huawei Technologies headquarters, in the Shenzhen Technology Development Park in Shenzhen, China (Source: Associated Press.)

Although Huawei is headquartered in China, it has established more than 100 international branch offices and 17 R&D facilities around the world. In addition to domestic centers in Shenzhen, Shanghai, Beijing, Nanjing, Xi'an, Chengdu, and Wuhan, Huawei has also established research facilities in Stockholm, Sweden; Dallas and Silicon Valley, United States; Bangalore, India; Ferbane in Offaly, Ireland; Moscow, Russia; Jakarta, Indonesia; and the Netherlands. [36] Its presence in the North American market has increased rapidly in recent years: From 2006 to 2010, Huawei has grown from 180 employees to more than 1,000. [37]

---

[34] Matthew Dalton, "Europe Raises Cry Over China Tech Exports," *Wall Street Journal*, October 5, 2010.

[35] Jonathan Stearns, "China Modem Makers May Face EU Anti-Subsidy Tariff," Bloomberg, September 16, 2010.

[36] Huawei Technologies Co., Ltd., the largest networking and telecommunications equipment supplier in the People's Republic of China. http://www.huawei.com.

[37] *Huawei Technologies (North America Region) Corporate Social Responsibility Report 2009-2010*, p. 19. http://www.huawei.com/na/en.

Figure 1: Huawei Technologies Offices in North America

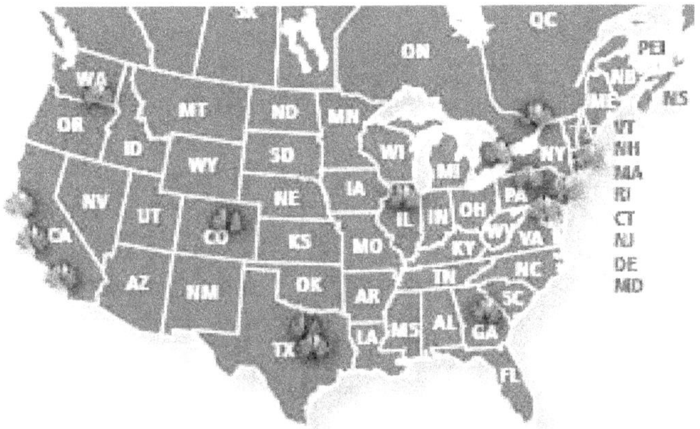

Source: Huawei Technologies (North America Region),
Corporate Social Responsibility Report 2009-2010, p. 19. http://www.huawei.com/na/en.

Huawei operates as an employee-owned company; however, its management structure is opaque, and media sources have raised questions about the true nature of the company's ownership. Huawei Technologies Co., Ltd., is itself a wholly owned subsidiary of Shenzhen Huawei Investment & Holding Co., Ltd. The company's employee shareholding program is managed by a shareholder body called the Union of Shenzhen Huawei Investment Holdings Co., Ltd., whose governing board is made up entirely of senior company officials. The company's shares are not freely traded but rather allocated to employees annually as incentives. Only employees within China can hold shares, and they must sell them back to the company if they leave Huawei's employ.[38]

Controversies Surrounding the Activities of Huawei

Allegations of Intellectual Property Piracy

Although Huawei has emerged as a highly successful company, it has been troubled by controversy over the years. Huawei has been accused in the past by its international competitors of extensive piracy and intellectual property theft: In one example, Cisco Systems, Inc., filed suit against Huawei and its American subsidiaries in 2003, alleging "wholesale infringement of Cisco's copyrights and misappropriation of Cisco's trade secrets... [to include] blatant and systematic copying of Cisco's router technology... [and] theft of Cisco's intellectual property by misappropriating and copying Cisco's source code, duplicating Cisco's user interface, and plagiarizing extensively from Cisco's user manuals."[39] The lawsuit was dropped in July 2004 after Huawei pledged to modify aspects of its computer products line.[40]

---

[38] Juha Saarinen, "Analysis: Who Really Owns Huawei?" *ITNews (Australia)*, May 28, 2010. http://www.itnews.com.au/News/175946,analysis-who-really-owns-huawei.aspx.

[39] United States District Court for the Eastern District of Texas (Marshall Division), Civil Action #2:03-CV-027 TJW, *Cisco Systems, Inc., and Cisco Technology, Inc. (Plaintiffs) vs. Huawei Technologies Co., Ltd., Huawei America, Inc., and Futurewei Technologies, Inc. (Defendants)*, "Cisco's Motion for Preliminary Injunction," dated February 5, 2003. http://newsroom.cisco.com/dlls/Cisco_Mot_for_PI.pdf.

[40] Cisco, Inc., press release, "Cisco Comments on Completion of Lawsuit Against Huawei," July 28, 2004. http://newsroom.cisco.com/dlls/2004/hd_072804.html.

15

Allegations of Threats to Communications Security

Huawei has also been the subject of questions regarding the nature of the company's management and its alleged close ties to the Chinese military. Some analysts have challenged the assertion that Huawei is an actor operating independently of the Chinese government. Noting that "both the [Chinese] government and the military tout Huawei as a national champion," an analysis by the RAND Corporation states that:

"...one does not need to dig too deeply to discover that [many Chinese information technology and telecommunications firms] are the public face for, sprang from, or are significantly engaged in joint research with state research institutes under the Ministry of Information Industry, defense-industrial corporations, or the military... Huawei was founded in 1988 by Ren Zhengfei, a former director of the PLA [People's Liberation Army] General Staff Department's Information Engineering Academy, which is responsible for telecom research for the Chinese military. Huawei maintains deep ties with the Chinese military, which serves a multi-faceted role as an important customer, as well as Huawei's political patron and research and development partner."[41]

Huawei founder Ren Zhengfei
Source: Google Images.

Aside from the controversy in the United States over the abortive effort by Huawei to purchase 3Com _(see pp. 28-30)_, media reports from other countries have also indicated concerns on the part of government security agencies in regard to Huawei's activities. British intelligence officials have reportedly warned government ministers of potential infrastructure threats emerging from communications equipment provided by Huawei to networks operated by British Telecom.[42] In Australia, intelligence officials have reportedly investigated alleged links between Chinese military officials and employees of Huawei's Australian offices.[43] In May 2010, Indian press reports revealed concern among intelligence officials about Huawei's activities in India, and the Indian communications ministry has placed limitations on the role of Huawei in India's communications networks.[44] In Taiwan, representatives of the opposition Democratic Progressive Party have also expressed concern over the expansion of Huawei into the island's telecom and network equipment markets, identifying this as a threat to Taiwan's security.[45]

---

[41] Evan Medeiros et al., _A New Direction for China's Defense Industry_ (Arlington, VA: RAND Corporation, 2005), pp. 217-218.
[42] See Michael Smith, "Spy Chiefs Fear Chinese Cyber Attack," _Sunday Times (London)_, March 29, 2009; and Alastair Jamieson, "Britain Could Be Shut Down by Hackers from China, Intelligence Experts Warn," _Telegraph (UK)_, March 29, 2009.
[43] Cameron Stewart, "Huawei in ASIO's Net," _Australian_, September 5, 2009.
[44] Bharti Jain, "Huawei Part of Chinese Spy Network, Says R&AW," _Economic Times (India)_, May 7, 2010.
[45] "Taiwan – Opposition Voices Concern over Huawei's Inroads," Open Source Center Report, June 10, 2010.

Huawei company officials have steadfastly rejected all such alleged security concerns related to the company's operations. Huawei officials have asserted the private nature of the company, calling it a Chinese embodiment of the "American Dream" and stressing the positive advantages of job creation at its facilities in the United States.[46] They also continue to maintain that "Huawei is privately held and 100 per cent owned by its employees" and that "[n]o other organizations, including the government, army or business hold stakes in Huawei."[47]

Allegations of Industrial Espionage

In July 2010, Motorola Inc. filed suit against Huawei in the U.S. District Court for the Northern District of Illinois, alleging a multiyear plot by Huawei's senior management to steal proprietary trade secrets from Motorola. The case had been in the making for some time but reportedly had been placed on hold while Motorola considered selling its network infrastructure business to Huawei.[48] However, on the heels of the July 19, 2010, announcement that Motorola was selling the majority of its wireless network infrastructure assets to Nokia Siemens Networks for $1.2 billion USD,[49] there was no longer any commercial incentive for Motorola to refrain from filing the lawsuit.

The lawsuit alleges that multiple Motorola employees – with two identified by name, Shaowei Pan and Hanjuan Jin – colluded with representatives of Huawei, including Huawei's founder Ren Zhengfei, to steal proprietary technology and pass it to Huawei. The alleged vehicle for some of these transfers was Lemko, a company founded by Shaowei Pan and other Motorola employees in 2002 while they were still employed by Motorola.[50] The matters in dispute in the civil case follow from a criminal case that first came to light in February 2007, when, according to allegations by U.S. government investigators:

"…one day after quitting Motorola, [Ms. Hanjuan] Jin was stopped at O'Hare airport with over 1,000 Motorola documents in her possession, both in hard copy and electronic format. A review of Motorola computer records showed that [Ms.] Jin accessed a large number of Motorola documents late at night. At the time she was stopped, Jin was traveling on a one-way ticket to China… [the charges against her] are based on evidence that Jin intended that the trade secrets she stole from Motorola would benefit the Chinese military."[51]

Mr. Pan allegedly held multiple meetings with Huawei officials from 2001 onwards, discussing Motorola's operations in international markets and his plans to establish Lemko as a company "independent of Motorola, Inc." Among the technology allegedly transferred was information about a Motorola base station – labeled "Motorola Confidential Property" – which Mr. Pan allegedly e-mailed to Huawei executives from his personal e-mail account in March 2003.[52]

---

[46] Statements made by Huawei representatives to staff of the U.S.-China Economic and Security Review Commission, July 7, 2009.

[47] Renai Lemay, "Huawei Denies 'Ludicrous' Espionage Claims," *ZDNet News Online,* December 18, 2008. http://www.zdnet.com.au/huawei-denies-ludicrous-espionage-claims-339293911.htm.

[48] Loretta Chao, "Motorola Suit Poses Challenges to Huawei's Success," *Wall Street Journal,* July 23, 2010.

[49] Motorola Inc. press release, "Nokia Siemens Networks to Acquire Certain Wireless Network Infrastructure Assets of Motorola for US $1.2 Billion," July 19, 2010. http://mediacenter.motorola.com/content/detail.aspx?ReleaseID=13055&NewsAreaId=2.

[50] Jamil Anderlini, "Motorola Claims Espionage in Huawei Lawsuit," *Financial Times,* July 22, 1010.

[51] U.S. Department of Justice, "Recent Espionage-Related Prosecutions Involving China," July 20, 2010. http://media.washingtonpost.com/wp-srv/politics/documents/spyprosecutions072010.pdf.

[52] Christopher Rhoads, "Motorola Claims Huawei Plot," *Wall Street Journal,* July 22, 2010.

Representatives of both Huawei and Lemko have denied the allegations, and the case is un-adjudicated as of the writing of this report.

Concerns about Huawei Expressed by Members of the U.S. Congress

Members of the U.S. Congress have weighed in on some of the controversies surrounding Huawei and have expressed concerns regarding the potential national security impacts of Huawei's efforts to purchase stakes in U.S. telecommunications companies. As one example, in October 2007 Representative Ileana Ros-Lehtinen (Florida, 18th District), along with 12 co-sponsors, introduced a draft House resolution (H.Res.730) that would have expressed opposition to Huawei's moves to acquire a stake in 3Com. [53] *(For further details on the abortive 3Com / Huawei deal, see pp. 28-30.)*

More recently, in August 2010 eight Members of the U.S. Senate (Sen. Jon Kyl, Arizona; Sen. Christopher Bond, Missouri; Sen. Richard Shelby, Alabama; Sen. James Inhofe, Oklahoma; Sen. Jim Bunning, Kentucky; Sen. Jeff Sessions, Alabama; Sen. Richard Burr, North Carolina; and Sen. Susan Collins, Maine) addressed a letter to senior officials of the Obama Administration (Secretary of the Treasury Timothy Geithner; Secretary of Commerce Gary Locke; Director of National Intelligence James Clapper; and Administrator of General Services Martha Johnson) that expressed concern over a pending deal by Huawei to supply equipment to Sprint Nextel *(see following page)*. The letter expressed concern that "Huawei's position as a supplier of Sprint Nextel could create substantial risk for US. companies and possibly undermine U.S. national security." The letter further offered a list of several questions about Huawei and its business activities and requested that the addressees provide responses to these questions.[54]

---

[53] H.Res.730, "Expressing the Sense of the House of Representatives Regarding the Planned Acquisition of a Minority Interest in 3Com by Affiliates of Huawei," 110th Cong., 1st sess., introduced October 10, 2007. Text available at *http://thomas.loc.gov/cgi-bin/query/z?c110:H.RES.730.*

[54] Letter from Sen. Jon Kyl, Arizona, Sen. Christopher Bond, Missouri, Sen. Richard Shelby, Alabama, Sen. James Inhofe, Oklahoma, Sen. Jim Bunning, Kentucky, Sen. Jeff Sessions, Alabama, Sen. Richard Burr, North Carolina, and Sen. Susan Collins, Maine, addressed to Secretary of the Treasury Timothy Geithner, Secretary of Commerce Gary Locke, Director of National Intelligence James Clapper, and Administrator of General Services Martha Johnson, dated August 18, 2010. The eleven specific questions directed to the addressees are as follows:

- *Does the United States government have unclassified information regarding Huawei's affiliation, if any, with the PLA? What does that information say about the affiliation/relationship, e.g., what control, if any, is exerted by the PLA on Huawei's operations?*
- *Is there any concern that Huawei, if it gained any measure of control over a U.S. contractor involved with sensitive U.S. government contracts, would present a national security threat for technology leakage or enhanced espionage against the United States? Please provide an unclassified response.*
- *Is the U.S. Treasury Department discussing or negotiating a deal to allow Huawei to acquire or invest in U.S. companies? What is the status of the negotiations? Will you agree to provide a briefing to Senators and their staffs on the present status?*
- *Has the Treasury Department included members of the intelligence community (IC) in its negotiations, if any, with Huawei? If yes, does the IC have a veto over any final negotiated product? Will you share with us and our staffs any IC analysis concerning the potential threat of Huawei obtaining any measure of control over a U.S. firm with sensitive contracts?*
- *What contracts with the Department of Defense (DOD) and the IC does Sprint Nextel have?*
- *Does Huawei currently supply companies with U.S. government contracts? If so, what are they?*
- *Have any goods provided to a U.S. government supplier by Huawei ever been found to contain suspect technology, such as intentional defects or "back doors" allowing remote entry?*
- *Please describe what, if any, a priori security review the General Services Administration conducts on technology (software or hardware) that the United States government purchases from overseas suppliers.*
- *Have U.S.-based employees of Huawei been granted security clearances by the U.S. government for access to classified information?*

Recent Unconsummated Huawei Deals, and Potential Huawei Deals on the Horizon

Huawei emerged into the spotlight of telecom industry analysts once again in spring and summer 2010, with speculation of potential new deals by Huawei in the U.S. telecom sector. In April 2010, an article in the *Financial Times* indicated that Huawei might be preparing a bid for the network infrastructure unit of Motorola, the U.S. mobile phone manufacturer. In an apparent attempt to head off the concerns surrounding the abortive 3Com deal, Huawei indicated that it would consider a "mitigation agreement," which would "show its willingness to co-operate with the US, [as] Alcatel of France did when it bought Lucent in 2006."[55] This came only two months after Motorola announced that it would be restructuring itself in 2011 into two separate companies--one that would operate its network infrastructure business, and one to handle its mobile phone and television set-top box business, with Huawei reportedly to pursue the former.[56] However, speculation on any such deal was ended in July 2010, when Motorola announced the purchase of its network infrastructure business by Nokia Siemens and filed suit against Huawei for alleged industrial espionage *(see text box on pp. 17-18).*

 It was also reported in spring 2010 that Huawei might be a potential suitor to buy into Harbinger Capital's planned Long-Term Evolution (LTE) network, which is likely to become a 4G (4th generation) technology standard.[57] *(See more on Huawei and LTE technology issues on pp. 45-46.)* Speculative reports have indicated that the hedge fund Harbinger Capital, which owns spectrum rights in the United States, could be looking for the cost efficiencies that Huawei can offer.[58] Huawei's known desire to expand in the smart phone business could also be satisfied by Harbinger's potentially expansive technology in a developed market.

In late July 2010, Huawei lost out in a bid to acquire the firm 2Wire. 2Wire, a U.S.-based broadband technology firm, was acquired by the British firm Pace for a reported $475 million, with the buyer reportedly interested in 2Wire's business in the residential broadband services market.[59] Huawei had reportedly offered a higher bid than Pace, but concerns over its ability to receive approval for the deal from the Committee on Foreign Investment in the United States (CFIUS) played a role in its failure to secure the deal. [60] *(For more on the committee and its review process, see pp. 30-33.)*

- *Please describe in detail any export licenses currently in review, or approved in the past five years, between any U.S. firm and Huawei.*
- *Has the Defense Intelligence Agency (DIA), Central Intelligence Agency (CIA), or National Security Agency (NSA) communicated with foreign intelligence agencies regarding their concerns, and vice versa, about Huawei's operations, affiliations and relationships?*

[55] Stephanie Kirchgaessner, "Huawei Tries To Calm US Fears," *Financial Times*, April 4, 2010. *http://www.ft.com/cms/s/2/44e5e210-400d-11df-8d23-00144feabdc.*

[56] *Trading Markets,* "Huawei Emerges As Potential Buyer of Motorola's Mobile Network, Report," March 17, 2010. *http://www.tradingmarkets.com/news/stock-alert/mot_huawei-emerges-as-potential-buyer-of-motorola-s-mobile-network-report-851479.html.*

[57] *C114,* "Harbinger Pioneers Open-Access LTE Network US," April 1, 2010. *http://www.cn-c114.net/575/a495001.html.*

[58] Stephanie Kirchgaessner, "Security Concerns Hold Back Huawei," *Financial Times,* July 8, 2010. *http://www.ft.com/cms/s/0/6fd9f072-8aba-11df-8e17-00144feab49a.html.*

[59] Paul Sandle, "Pace Buys U.S. Broadband Co 2Wire for $475 Mln," Reuters, July 26, 2010. *http://www.reuters.com/article/idUSTRE66P1UL20100726.*

[60] Stephanie Kirchgaessner and Helen Thomas, "US Divided on How to Tackle Huawei," *Financial Times,* July 29, 2010.

Finally, in what arguably has emerged as Huawei's most high-profile deal of 2010, media reports first disclosed in July 2010 that Huawei was bidding to sell equipment for an expansion of the wireless broadband network of Sprint Nextel, America's third-largest mobile operator.[61] Huawei's leading partner in this proposed deal is Amerilink Telecom Corporation, a company staffed largely by former employees of Sprint Nextel. To date, Amerilink is acting primarily as a distributor for equipment made by Huawei and as a consultant for Huawei's efforts further to penetrate the U.S. market.[62] These efforts have been the subject of controversy: In August 2010, eight Members of the U.S. Senate addressed a letter to senior officials of the Obama Administration that expressed concern over the pending deal by Huawei to supply equipment to Sprint Nextel *(see text box on page 18)*.[63]

A trio of prominent public figures is associated with Amerilink: its founder, William Owens, is a retired U.S. Navy admiral and a former vice chairman of the U.S. Joint Chiefs of Staff;[64] and in 2010, the company recruited former U.S. House of Representatives Democratic Leader Richard Gephardt and former World Bank President James Wolfensohn to serve as members of its board of directors.[65] Amerilink representatives have been active in engaging U.S. officials about the proposed deal with Sprint Nextel; they reportedly have also sought to mitigate concerns about Huawei's hardware by offering that Amerilink certify it for network security purposes.[66]

Security concerns expressed by government officials are believed to be a factor in Sprint Nextel's decision in November 2010 to exclude Huawei Technologies Ltd. and ZTE Corporation from final consideration as equipment suppliers for upgrades to its cellular networks, a deal worth billions of dollars.[67]

Concerns Regarding Potential Network Penetration by PRC Intelligence Agencies

The *Washington Post* has reported that representatives of the National Security Agency (NSA) contacted senior executives of AT&T late in 2009 to warn them against purchasing equipment from Huawei. According to the *Post* article, "The NSA called AT&T because of fears that China's intelligence agencies could insert digital trapdoors into Huawei's technology that would serve as secret listening posts in the U.S. communications network." [68] At the time, AT&T was taking bids from potential suppliers for its planned next-generation LTE phone network. AT&T has not made any public comment about the reported messages from the NSA, but it did announce in

---

[61] Paul Taylor and Stephanie Kirchgaessner, "Huawei in Drive to Land Big US Deal," *Financial Times,* July 8, 2010; and Reuters, "China's Huawei Bids for Sprint Equipment Deal: Report," July 8, 2010. *http://www.reuters.com/article/idUSTRE6680E920100709.*

[62] Loretta Chao and Paul Ziobro, "Huawei Enlists an Ex-Sprint Team," *Wall Street Journal,* August 24, 2010.

[63] Letter from Sen. Jon Kyl, Arizona, Sen. Christopher Bond, Missouri, Sen. Richard Shelby, Alabama, Sen. James Inhofe, Oklahoma, Sen. Jim Bunning, Kentucky, Sen. Jeff Sessions, Alabama, Sen. Richard Burr, North Carolina, and Sen. Susan Collins, Maine, addressed to Secretary of the Treasury Timothy Geithner, Secretary of Commerce Gary Locke, Director of National Intelligence James Clapper, and Administrator of General Services Martha Johnson, dated August 18, 2010.

[64] Team." *Prometheus. http://prometheusasia.com/team.html*; and Loretta Chao and Paul Ziobro, "Huawei Enlists an Ex-Sprint Team," *Wall Street Journal,* August 24, 2010.

[65] Spencer Ante and Shayndi Raice, "Dignitaries Come on Board to Ease Huawei Into U.S.," *Wall Street Journal,* September 21, 2010.

[66] John Pomfret, "Between U.S. and China, a Trust Gap," *Washington Post,* October 8, 2010.

[67] Joann S. Lublin and Shayndi Raice, "Security Fears Kill Chinese Bid in U.S.," *Wall Street Journal,* November 5, 2010.

[68] John Pomfret, "Between U.S. and China, a Trust Gap," *Washington Post,* October 8, 2010.

February 2010 that it had selected Ericsson and Alcatel-Lucent as its equipment and service suppliers for the network upgrade.[69]

Assuming that the account of the NSA warning is true, the PRC intelligence entity of greatest concern would likely be the Third Department of the People's Liberation Army General Staff Department, China's leading signals intelligence agency. The Third Department is reportedly the largest of all of China's intelligence services,[70] offering the PRC:

"by far, the most extensive SIGINT capability of any nation in the Asia-Pacific region. The Chinese operate several dozen SIGINT ground stations deployed throughout China. There they monitor signals from Russia, Taiwan, Japan, South Korea, India, and Southeast Asia. Signals from U.S. military units located in the region are of significant interest to these monitoring stations, and a large SIGINT facility at Hainan Island is principally concerned with monitoring U.S. naval activities in the South China Sea."[71]

Aside from the collection of communications information, the Third Department also likely bears primary responsibility within the PLA for computer network exploitation (i.e., "cyber espionage") operations. The Third Department is also assessed to have a complementary relationship with the Fourth Department of the PLA General Staff Department, which takes a leading role in computer network attack operations.[72] *(For further discussion of PRC intelligence agencies and their functions, see the Commission's* 2009 Annual Report to Congress, *chapter 2, section 3, "China's Human Espionage Activities that Target the United States, and the Resulting impacts on U.S. National Security.")*

ZTE CORPORATION

ZTE Company Logo

[69] Ruth Bender and Gustav Sandstrom, "2nd UPDATE: Ericsson, Alcatel Get 4G Network Deal From AT&T," *Foxbusiness.com,* February 10, 2010. *http://www.foxbusiness.com/story/markets/industries/telecom/nd-update-ericsson-alcatel-g-network-deal-att/.*

[70] U.S.-China Economic and Security Review Commission, *Annual Report to Congress 2009* (Washington, DC: U.S. Government Printing Office, November 2009), p. 153. A firm open-source estimate on the number of personnel in the Third Department is not available. For two sources, see Howard DeVore, *China's Intelligence and Internal Security Forces* (Alexandria, VA: Jane's Information Group, 1999), p. 48; and Nicholas Eftimiades, *Chinese Intelligence Operations* (Annapolis, MD: Naval Institute Press, 1994), p. 46. A figure of 20,000 personnel is provided by Mr. DeVore. A figure of 130,000 is provided in Kan Chung-kuo, "Intelligence Agencies Exist in Great Numbers, Spies Are Present Everywhere; China's Major Intelligence Departments Fully Exposed," *'Chien Shao'* (Frontline), January 1, 2006. OSC ID: CPP20060110510011.*www.open source.gov.*

[71] Interagency OPSEC Support Staff, *Intelligence Threat Handbook* (2004), p.75. *http://www.fas.org/irp/threat/handbook/supplement.pdf.*

[72] U.S.-China Economic and Security Review Commission, *Annual Report to Congress 2009* (Washington, DC: U.S. Government Printing Office, November 2009), pp. 153 and 172. James Mulvenon, "PLA Computer Network Operations," in *Beyond the Strait: PLA Missions Other Than Taiwan,* eds. Roy Kamphausen, David Lai, and Andrew Scobell (Carlisle, PA: U.S. Army War College Strategic Studies Institute, 2009); Northrop Grumman Corporation, "Capability of the People's Republic of China to Conduct Cyber Warfare and Computer Network Exploitation" (contracted research paper for the U.S.-China Economic and Security Review Commission, June 2009), p. 19. *http://www.uscc.gov/researchpapers/2009/NorthropGrumman/ PRC/Cyber/Paper/FINAL/Approved%20Report/16Oct2009.pdf.*

Another major player in the Chinese networking market is ZTE Corporation [*Zhongxing Tongxun Gufen Youxian Gongsi* /中兴通讯股份有限公司], a telecommunications company based in Shenzhen. One of the first Chinese telecom equipment providers to pursue business in overseas markets, ZTE now has about 62,000 employees, about 107 representative offices around the world, and 15 research labs throughout North America, Europe, and Asia. ZTE states that 34 percent of its workforce and 10 percent of its revenues are dedicated to R&D. [73] Since 1996, the company has provided products and services to 135 countries and regions, serving major telecom operators in the Asia Pacific region, South Asia, North America, Europe, Latin America, Africa, and the Commonwealth of Independent States. [74]

ZTE was established in 1985 from "a handful of state-owned companies affiliated with the Ministry of Aerospace Industry." [75] Though the company is publicly listed on the Shenzhen stock exchange and the Hong Kong stock exchange, government-affiliated entities appear to retain a majority share of its stock. [76] Over the last decade, ZTE has steadily increased its global market share among telecom equipment makers. [77] This increase is mostly due to the company's ability to focus on networking gear, as opposed to phones, and its dedication to delivering equipment that is low cost but reliable. By 2007, ZTE had already become one of the world's top ten mobile phone makers, joining the ranks of telecom giants Nokia and Samsung. ZTE's annual income in 2009 was US $486.4 million [78] and, despite the global downturn, the company's growth is projected to be strong.

Among western countries, ZTE is a quiet giant, supplying handsets to operators without branding them under its own name. ZTE also has focused mainly on customers in developing countries who require cost-effective telecom solutions and whose countries lack sophisticated infrastructure. ZTE is highly specialized in CDMA [code division multiple access] technology and is willing to customize products for clients. As a result, ZTE's export sales account for a majority of its revenues.

ZTE has established strategic cooperation agreements with leading telecom giants such as Portugal Telecom, France Telecom, Alcatel-Lucent, Ericsson, and Nortel in next generation network and mobile systems, with Hutchison in 3G (3rd generation), and with Marconi in optical transmission systems. The company has also established joint laboratory partnerships with Texas Instruments, Intel, Agere Systems, HHNEC, IBM, Microsoft (China), Qualcomm, Huahong NEC, and Tsinghua University. [79] As Chinese products achieve greater acceptability

---

[73] ZTE- Corporate information. *http://zte.com.cn*.

[74] Zhong Xing Telecommunication Equipment Company Limited, "ZTE Corporation," a publicly owned Chinese corporation that designs and manufactures telecommunications and networking equipment and systems. *http://wwwen.zte.com.cn/en*.

[75] *Bloomberg Business Week*, "A Global Telecom Titan Called… ZTE?" March 7, 2005. *http://www.businessweek.com/magazine/content/05_10/b3923071.htm.*

76 A press clipping from 2006 posted on a ZTE company website states that "Although a listed company, [ZTE] is still very much a state-owned enterprise (SOE), with more than 69 percent of its shares owned by government-affiliated entities." See China Online News, "Why Zhongxing is the CDMA Leader in China," September 13, 2006. Posted on the ZTE "Press Center" webpage at *http://wwwen.zte.com.cn/en/press_center/press_clipping/200106/t20010622_156932.html* .

77 *Economist*, "Silent Mode; ZTE," October 16, 2008. *http://ezproxy.library.nyu.edu:2076/us/lnacademic/results/docview/docview.do?docLinkInd=true&risb=21_T96643512 10&format=GNBFI&sort=RELEVANCE&startDocNo=1&resultsUrlKey=29_T9664351222&cisb=22_T9664351221&tre eMax=true&treeWidth=0&csi=7955&docNo=7.*

78 "Company Description: ZTE Corporation," Hoovers Inc., July 1, 2010.

[79] ZTE Corporation. *http://wwwen.zte.com.cn/en/about/corporate_information.*

with American consumers – just as Japanese products began to be accepted in the 1960s and 1970s – price points and dependability tend to mute country-of-origin concerns.

THE ROLE OF HUAWEI AND ZTE IN THE U.S. MARKET

The telecommunications sector may be one of the most interconnected sectors of business between U.S. companies and Chinese companies, and this trend is continuing. For example, Huawei has expanded its facilities in Plano, Texas, to become its new North American headquarters,[80] and press reports in 2009 indicated that Huawei plans to expand its workforce to nearly 1,100 people within the United States and Canada.[81]

Huawei and ZTE are now among the top six global wireless equipment manufacturers, eclipsing, in some product categories, Alcatel-Lucent, Nortel (now in bankruptcy and being sold off in pieces), Cisco, and Motorola.[82] *(For more on Huawei's dealings with Nortel, see pp. 54-56.)* In many product classes, Huawei and ZTE rank in the top three of manufacturers, with Huawei rapidly moving toward number one in providing a full range of wireless networking equipment and handsets (often relabeled under other wireless network manufacturer brand names).

Huawei and ZTE have developed, manufactured, and sold technologically savvy, lower-cost, good-quality products in market niches.[83] While Huawei has had many product entries in the wireless market, its extraordinary range of product offerings supports almost every meaningful segment of telecommunications network architecture. Both Huawei and ZTE have typically introduced their mobile phones into the United States and other new market spaces through relabeling for companies like Verizon Wireless and T-Mobile.

Along with other technology equipment, as the manufacture of mobile phone handsets and associated software moves to offshore outsourcers, security could be compromised. Although there are no readily available case studies where this has actually happened, there is a potential risk of jeopardizing one of the most widely used forms of communications in the United States. Of most interest are Huawei's product uses that have deep vertical penetrations across all aspects of wireless, long haul, deep sea fiber, software, security, and cable networks.

Examples of U.S. Market Penetration by Chinese Telecom Companies

- **July 2007**: An infrastructure agreement between Huawei and Leap Wireless was announced.[84]
- **March 2009**: Huawei became a supplier to Cox Communications for its wireless network, giving the company a major foothold in cable and wireless[85] in the United States.

---

[80] "Huawei to Add Hundreds of Tech Jobs," *Texas Business Journal*, May 1, 2009.

[81] "Huawei to Add Hundreds of Tech Jobs," *Texas Business Journal*, May 1, 2009.

[82] The original research for this report was performed in 2009, therefore some data have changed. The website "Seeking Alpha" recently reported that Huawei's expansion into the international router market is eating into Cisco's core router business and that "Huawei is currently the 2nd largest telecom equipment supplier globally with a share of 20% as of Q3 2009." See "China's Huawei: Margins, Market Share and Cisco's Router Business," *SeekingAlpha*.com, April 12, 2010. *http://seekingalpha.com/article/198323-china-s-huawei-margins-market-share-and-cisco-s-router-business*.

[83] *Wall Street Journal,* "China's Telecom Gear Makers, Once Laggards at Home, Pass Foreign Rivals,",April 10,2010.

[84] Fierce Wireless, "Huawei to deploy CDMA 2000 infrastructure for Cricket Communications," July 11, 2007.

- **March 2009**: Announcement was made that Huawei had deployed a 3G wireless network in Chicago for Cricket Communications, a subsidiary of Leap Wireless.[86]
- **August 2009**: Clearwire, LLC, announced a partnership with Huawei for its wireless communications network.[87] (Clearwire and Sprint Nextel merged in 2008.[88])
- **March 2010**: ZTE, Chinese manufacturer of mobile phone handsets and infrastructure, announced its expectation to sell phones through major U.S. operators in the second half of the year.[89]

In 2008, Huawei announced a joint venture with Symantec, a U.S. manufacturer of network security products. The Huawei Symantec joint venture is likely complementary to Huawei's continued range of product offerings for telecommunications and network services.[90] It is natural for communications manufacturers to gravitate to the network security space. However, as foreign companies occupy a greater role in this field, there is an increased risk for compromised network security products to be implemented unnoticed in sensitive infrastructures. *(For more on the Huawei Symantec joint venture, see p. 47.)*

On September 29, 2008, a press release posted on Nokia's website announced that the Nokia Siemens Networks and Huawei, with its affiliates, had agreed upon a patent license for standards-essential patents. This will cover the worldwide use of all standards-essential patents of all parties, including GSM (global system for mobile communications), WCDMA (wideband code division multiple access), CDMA2000, optical networking, datacom, and WiMAX, and will affect mobile devices, infrastructure, and services.[91] On March 30, 2009, the Huawei website announced that Huawei had been selected to provide end-to-end cellular solution and services to Cox Communications. Cox, the third-largest cable provider in the United States, will launch its 3G wireless network utilizing Huawei's LTE (3GPP [partnership project] 4G technology)-ready SingleRAN solution and industry-leading 3900 Series base stations.[92] In 2008, Huawei offered its handset unit for sale to private equity firms including Bain Capital, Blackstone, TPG (formerly Texas Pacific Group), Kohlberg Kravis Roberts, Warburg Pincus, and Carlyle Group for $4 billion.[93] The offer was later pulled, reportedly due to the condition of financial markets.

THE MAJOR CHINESE DOMESTIC TELECOM CORPORATIONS

While Huawei and ZTE have been among the most active Chinese telecoms in their overseas investments and business activities, China also has other telecom companies, which primarily service the domestic market. The three most prominent, which are all state owned, are listed below.

---

[85] Light Reading, Cable Digital News, "Cox, Huawei Make Wireless Connection," March 30, 2009.
[86] Huawei Press Release, March 2009.
[87] Light Reading Mobile, "Clearwire Confirms Huawei Deal," August 11, 2009.
[88] *InformationWeek,* "FCC Approves Sprint Clearwire Merger," November 5, 2008.
[89] Fierce Wireless, March 29, 2010.
[90] Symantec Press Release, "Huawei and Symantec Commence Joint Venture," February 5, 2008.
[91] "Nokia Siemens Partners with Huawei," September 29, 2008. The agreement covers worldwide use of all standards essential patents of all parties. *http://news.softpedia.com/news/Nokia-Siemens-Partners-With-Huawei-94374.shtml.*
[92] Huawei website, March 20,2009. *http://www.huawei.com/news/view.do?id=10799&cid=42*.
[93] Michael Flaherty and Vinicy Chan, "Private Equity Firms Line Up for Huawei Unit Sale," Reuters, June 5, 2008. *http://in.reuters.com/article/idINHKG31043120080605.*

China Mobile

China Mobile Ltd. [*Zhongguo Yidong Tongxin* - 中国移动通信] is currently the world's largest mobile telephone operator.[94] China Mobile provides cellular and value-added mobile services to 31 provinces of mainland China and Hong Kong. With approximately 548 million subscribers (as of May 31, 2010) and over 70 percent of the Chinese cellular market, China Mobile is considered a central state-owned enterprise by the Chinese government.[95] The company has historically operated on a GSM network, but in 2009 it rolled out its home-grown 3G network operating on a time division synchronous code division multiple access (TD-SCDMA) network.[96] China Mobile is currently listed on both the New York Stock Exchange (NYSE:CHL) as well as the Hong Kong stock exchange (941:HKG). Its operating revenue in 2009 was renminbi (RMB) 518.08 billion.[97]

Founded in 1988 as Guangdong Mobile, the commercial mobile telephone network was initially operated by the provincial government of Guangdong for use by high-level officials of state-owned enterprises and high-ranking government officials.[98] By 1997, the Chinese government sought to restructure the telecommunications industry by consolidating provincial telecom corporations. In 2000, the government merged Guangdong Mobile and the telephone operator of Zhejiang into a subsidiary of China Telecom Hong Kong BVI, called China Mobile Ltd. To date, the company is still directly controlled by the government, which has a 74.22 percent equity stake through China Mobile (Hong Kong) Limited, which is wholly owned by the government as an arm of China Mobile Communications Corporation, also government owned.[99]

China Telecom

China Telecom [*Zhongguo Dianxin* / 中国电信] is the largest fixed-line telecommunications operator and broadband service provider in the world.[100] It is one of the leading providers of broadband access services in the Chinese market and has a strong foothold in the residential market.[101] Considered one of the top three state-backed telecommunications companies in

[94]China Mobile Limited, "Operation Data." *http://www.chinamobileltd.com/about.php?menu=1.*

[95] Bruce Einhorn, "China Mobile Is Counting on Android," *Business Week,* August 20, 2009. *http://www.businessweek.com/globalbiz/content/aug2009/gb20090820_505265.htm.*

[96] *New York Times*, "China Mobile's 2nd Quarter Profit Slips," August 21, 2009. *http://ezproxy.library.nyu.edu:2076/us/lnacademic/results/docview/docview.do?docLinkInd=true&risb=21_T97696080 77&format=GNBFI&sort=RELEVANCE&startDocNo=1&resultsUrlKey=29_T9769608080&cisb=22_T9769608079&tre eMax=true&treeWidth=0&selRCNodeID=37&nodeStateId=411en_US,1,36&docsInCategory=5&csi=6742&docNo=1.*

[98] *Financial Times*, "China Mobile Ltd.," July 19, 2010. *http://markets.ft.com/tearsheets/businessProfile.asp?s=941:HKG.*

[99] *Business & Company Resource Center: Novel NY*, "China Mobile Ltd." *http://ezproxy.library.nyu.edu:2081/servlet/BCRC?rsic=PK&rcp=CO&vrsn=unknown&locID=nysl_me_nyuniv&srchtp= cmp&cc=1&c=1&mode=c&ste=74&tbst=tsCM&tab=4&ccmp=China+Mobile+Ltd.&tcp=china+mobile&n=25&docNum= I2501313383&bConts=13119.*

[100] *Economist*, "Strait Deals; Chinese Investment," May 9, 2009. *http://ezproxy.library.nyu.edu:2076/us/lnacademic/results/docview/docview.do?docLinkInd=true&risb=21_T97690899 16&format=GNBFI&sort=RELEVANCE&startDocNo=1&resultsUrlKey=29_T9769089925&cisb=22_T9769089924&tre eMax=true&treeWidth=0&selRCNodeID=26&nodeStateId=411en_US,1,23&docsInCategory=5&csi=7955&docNo=2.;* and Doug Young, "China Mobile Growth Prospects Improve," Reuters, March 18, 2010. *http://www.reuters.com/article/idUSTRE62H0IU20100318.*

[101] China Telecom, "Company Overview. *http://www.chinatelecom-h.com/eng/company/company_overview.htm.*

[102] Frederick Yeung, "China Telecom Challenges Leader," *South China Morning Post (Hong Kong)*, November 18, 2008. *http://ezproxy.library.nyu.edu:2076/us/lnacademic/results/docview/docview.do?docLinkInd=true&risb=21_T97707883*

China, China Telecom is the leader in fixed-line networks but is currently the third-largest wireless operator (behind China Mobile and China Unicom), with only 56 million subscribers.[102] The company was listed on the New York Stock Exchange (NYSE:CHA) and the Hong Kong Stock Exchange (HK:728) in November 2002, with an initial public offering of approximately USD $1.3 billion.

China Telecom was established in 1994 by the Chinese government to oversee the nation's public telecommunications operations. By 1997, China Telecom had become the second-largest fixed-line telephone network in the world, with over 100 million subscribers.[103] In 2008, China Telecom acquired the CDMA network of China Unicom, the third-largest telecommunications firm in China, a move intended to boost the mobile phone operations of China Telecom.[104] The company is still largely subject to policy changes in the Chinese government: China Telecommunications Corporation, a state-owned enterprise, owns a 70.89 percent stake in China Telecom.

China Unicom

China Unicom [*Zhongguo Liantong* / 中国联通] is China's second-largest telecom company, after China Mobile. It is an integrated telecommunications operator offering mobile voice, value-added, fixed-line voice, and broadband services. In 2008, the company had over 273 million subscribers and total assets of around RMB 500.09 billion.[105] China Unicom is the only Chinese telecom to be traded on the New York Stock Exchange (NYSE:CHU), the Hong Kong Stock Exchange (SEHK:0762), and the Shanghai Stock Exchange (SSE:600050). Even so, the company is a state-owned enterprise, with China Netcom Group Corporation (BVI) Limited and China Unicom (BVI) Limited, both state-owned firms, as the two largest shareholders.

Created in 1994 with the permission of the State Council, China Unicom was part of a government reform aimed at the domestic telecom industry to discourage monopolies.[106] For many years, the company mainly operated in northern China and eventually became the official partner of the 2008 Beijing Olympic Games for fixed communications services. In 2009, China Unicom sold its CDMA mobile assets to China Telecom and merged with China Netcom. The merger resulted in an acquisition of fixed-line businesses in 21 provinces in southern China for RMB 4.63 billion.[107] In recent years, it has formed strategic alliances with such companies as

---

63&format=GNBFI&sort=RELEVANCE&startDocNo=1&resultsUrlKey=29_T9770788366&cisb=22_T9770788365&treeMax=true&treeWidth=0&csi=11314&docNo=2.

[103] Toh Han Shih, "China Telecom Expects Earnings Rebound," *South China Morning Post (Hong Kong)*, March 23, 2010. *http://ezproxy.library.nyu.edu:2076/us/lnacademic/results/docview/docview.do?docLinkInd=true&risb=21_T97705640 60&format=GNBFI&sort=RELEVANCE&startDocNo=1&resultsUrlKey=29_T9770564065&cisb=22_T9770564064&treeMax=true&treeWidth=0&csi=11314&docNo=9.*

[104] *Business & Company: Resource Center,* "China Telecom Corporation Ltd." *http://ezproxy.library.nyu.edu:2081/servlet/BCRC?vrsn=unknown&locID=nysl_me_nyuniv&srchtp=glbc&cc=2&c=1&mode=c&ste=74&tbst=tsCM&tab=4&ccmp=China+Telecom+Corporation+Ltd.&mst=china+telecom&n=25&docNum=I2501151876&bConts=9023.*

[104] *Economist,* 'Rewired; Telecoms in China," May 31, 2008. *http://ezproxy.library.nyu.edu:2076/us/lnacademic/results/docview/docview.do?docLinkInd=true&risb=21_T97704295 90&format=GNBFI&sort=BOOLEAN&startDocNo=1&resultsUrlKey=29_T9770429596&cisb=22_T9770429595&treeMax=true&treeWidth=0&selRCNodeID=9&nodeStateId=411en_US,1,8&docsInCategory=3&csi=7955&docNo=2.*

[105] China Unicom, "Corporate Profile."

[106] China Unicom, "Our History." *http://eng.chinaunicom.com/about/Eng_qywh/index.html.*

[107] Benjamin Scent, "Unicom in 6.43B Yuan Deal," *Standard (London),* December 17, 2008.

Spanish telecommunications operator Telefónica to swap stock as well as jointly purchase mobile networks and phones.[108]

State-Directed Personnel Shuffling and Restructuring at PRC Telecom Corporations

While questions may circulate about the extent of PRC state influence over the nominally private companies Huawei and ZTE, there is far less ambiguity regarding China's major domestic telecom corporations, all of which are directly state controlled. With these companies, the controlling hand of the state is very clear. The Chinese government exercises extensive command over the management and operations of these companies, as illustrated in the examples below:

2004

In October 2004, the Chinese government abruptly shuffled the senior management of the three "China" telecoms: a senior executive from China Unicom was made the new head of China Mobile, a former China Mobile vice president was appointed to head China Telecom, and the head executive of China Telecom was moved to China Unicom.[109] The sudden personnel moves had been directed by the Central Organization Department of the Chinese Communist Party,[110] and ignored the nominal legal and fiduciary responsibilities of the corporate boards to select the managing officials of each company.[111] It shocked many shareholders and industry analysts and even drew criticism from the business journal *Caijing*, one of the bolder voices in the Chinese media.[112] It was, as one author has said, "the equivalent of the CEO [chief executive officer] of AT&T being moved without notice to head its domestic US competitor, Verizon, with the Verizon chief being appointed to run Sprint, at a time when the three companies were locked in a bruising battle on price and industry standards."[113]

2008

Another dramatic shuffle of personnel, and an accompanying state-mandated restructuring of the telecom sector, occurred in May 2008. At that time, new appointments were made to (1) the positions of company president and party secretary at both China Mobile and China Telecom; (2) the president of China Tietong [*Zhongguo Tietong Gongsi* / 中国铁通 公司], the vice president of China Unicom, and the vice president of China Unicom were all transferred to China Mobile; and (3) the vice president of China Unicom, and the head of the CCP Discipline Inspection Team of China Unicom, were transferred to China Telecom.[114] The restructuring also mandated the merging of China Mobile and the smaller China Tietong and for China Unicom to be divided, with its CDMA network sold off to China Telecom and its GSM network business merged into China Netcom.[115]

---

[108]Kevin O'Brien, "Telefónica and China Unicom Deepen Links," *International Herald Tribune,* September 7, 2009.

[109] Kathrin Hille, "China Mobile in Board Shake Up," *Financial Times,* May 31, 2010.

[110] Richard McGregor, *The Party: The Secret World of China's Communist Rulers* (New York: Harper Collins, 2010), pp. 84-89; and Kathrin Hille, "China Mobile in Board Shake Up," *Financial Times,* May 31, 2010.

[111] Richard McGregor, *The Party: The Secret World of China's Communist Rulers* (New York; Harper Collins, 2010), p. 85.

[112] *Caijing,* "The Telecoms Reshuffle: More Harm Than Good," November 15, 2004.

[113] Richard McGregor, *The Party: The Secret World of China's Communist Rulers* (New York: Harper Collins, 2010), p. 84.

[114] ChinaTechNews.com, "China's Telecom Restructuring Plan Finally Announced," May 26, 2008. *http://www.chinatechnews.com/2008/05/26/6787-chinas-telecom-restructuring-plan-finally-announced.*

[115] Wang Xing, "Jury Out on Dramatic Telecom Restructure," *China Daily,* May 24, 2008.

2010
Another government-directed management shake-up in the telecom sector was seen in May 2010, when Wang Jianzhou, the chief executive of China Mobile, was removed from his position as general manager and appointed to chair a newly established board of directors for the company. Mr. Wang was also appointed party secretary of China Mobile's Communist Party committee. He was succeeded as general manager by Li Yue, the company's vice president. China Mobile indicated that the move had been directed once again by the Central Organization Department, and in phraseology evocative of internal CCP discourse, indicated that it was part of a plan to "make the company's management strategy more scientific and regulated." The *Financial Times* commented that the sudden reshuffle at China Mobile "left observers confused… underscoring the opaque nature of China's state enterprises."[116]

HUAWEI AND 3-COM: A CLASSIC EXAMPLE OF CHINA'S FORAYS INTO THE U.S. MARKET VIA JOINT VENTURE AND ACQUISITION

3Com Corporation was a major American telecommunications company that invented, manufactured, integrated, and implemented network infrastructure products and developed supporting service models throughout the small, medium, and (to a lesser degree) large enterprise markets of North America.[117] 3Com Corporation and Huawei formed a joint venture in 2003 for the purpose of developing data communications products. In 2006, 3Com bought out the Huawei stake in the joint venture. In 2007, Bain Capital and Huawei made a $2.2 billion dollar bid for 3Com, which was eventually abandoned due to security concerns on the part of the U.S. government.[118] *(See more below.)* In November 2009, 3Com announced its acquisition by Hewlett-Packard for $2.7 billion.[119]

As a manufacturer of routers, switches, and hubs, 3Com had equipment that was often found in the heart of telecommunications networks and that provided connectivity to some of the most secure areas of infrastructures. Nevertheless, despite being a pioneer in the technology of Internet protocol (IP) communications and networking, 3Com lacked brand identity and penetration into the large enterprise market segment due to the presence of more well-established vendors. Strategic decisions to avoid affiliation with IP telephony technology platforms by some companies, such as Microsoft, further constrained 3Com's ability to penetrate further into its chosen markets.

Within two weeks after announcing a net loss of $18.7 million for its first quarter 2008 revenues, 3Com said that it was being acquired by Bain Capital Partners LLC. Bain had previously handled numerous large technology-based buyouts, to include the takeover of Texas Instruments Inc.'s sensors and controls division.[120] Bain's offer for the deal was $2.2 billion, with Huawei Tech Investment Co. Ltd. (Hong Kong) to acquire a minority 16.5 percent interest worth $363 million. Huawei Tech Investment Co. Ltd. is a wholly owned subsidiary of Huawei Technologies Co. Ltd. (Hong Kong), 3Com's former joint venture partner in the H3C venture.

---

[116] Kathrin Hille, "China Mobile in Board Shake Up," *Financial Times,* May 31, 2010.

[117] 3-Com website section on corporate history. *http://www.3-Com.com*.

[118] Reuters, "Opposition Leads Bain to Call Off 3Com Deal," March 21, 2008. *http://www.nytimes.com/2008/03/21/technology/21com.html*; and *Cajing China (English version),* "The 3Com Deal, Behind the Security Flap," October 23, 2007.

[119] Bloomberg.com, "3-Com Agrees to $2.2 billion dollar purchase," September 28, 2007.

[120] Texas Instruments press release, "TI Completes Sale of Sensor Control Business to Bain Capital," April 26, 2006.

However, the intended deal between Huawei and 3Com fell afoul of the U.S. government interagency Committee on Foreign Investment in the United States (CFIUS), which investigated the deal on national security grounds. *(For further information on the CFIUS process, see pp. 30-33.)* Among the alleged concerns were (1) that Huawei had links to the Chinese military; and (2) that Tipping Point, a subordinate unit of 3Com, provides network security products and services to the Department of Defense (DOD) and a number of other federal agencies.[121] Following failure to negotiate a "mitigation agreement" to answer government concerns, Bain announced in March 2008 that it was backing out of the deal.[122]

A Timeline History of 3Com [123]

- 1979: Founded by Robert Metcalfe (inventor of Ethernet) in 1979.
- 1984: Goes public.
- 1987: Acquires Bridge Communications.
- 1997: Acquires U.S. Robotics (modem manufacturer and owner of Palm, Inc.).
- 1999: 3Com acquires NBX and achieves much progress in initial validation and adoption of VOIP (Voice Over Internet Protocol).
- 2000: Reaches its peak market value of $25.8 billion listed on the NASDAQ.[124]
  -- Exits the high-end router business due to strong competition from Cisco; many of 3Com's larger customers feel abandoned by their vendor of choice.
  -- Buys Kerbango and attempts new business entry into Internet radio market but abandons the initiative in less than a year.
  -- U.S. Robotics & Palm are spun off and become separate again.
- 2003: Joint venture with Huawei to create H3C. Combined research on routers, switches, wireless networking, security, VOIP, network management systems, and other enterprise and small office home office SOHO (small office home office) -level solutions. 3Com gains access to Asian markets, and Huawei gains access to U.S. and European markets.
  -- Sells ComWorks Corporation to UT StarCom.[125]
- 2005: After the DotCom bust, shares of stock fall in value from an adjusted record of $21.89 to $2.96 per share.
- 2006: Generates nearly 37.6 percent of revenues from Europe, Middle East, and Africa; 31.3 percent from North America; 22.1 percent from Asia/Pacific; and 9 percent from Central and South America.
- 2007: Juniper Networks (carrier-level telecom and network hardware manufacturer) expresses an interest in buying the H3C joint venture.

---

[121] Reuters, "Opposition Leads Bain to Call Off 3Com Deal," March 21, 2008. *http://www.nytimes.com/2008/03/21/technology/21com.html* ; and Steven R. Weisman, "Sale of 3Com to Huawei is Derailed by U.S. Security Concerns," *New York Times*, February 21, 2008. *http://www.nytimes.com/2008/02/21/business/worldbusiness/21iht-3com.1.10258216.html*. See also Tipping Point website, "U.S. Federal Government Solutions." *http://www.tippingpoint.com/solutions_federal.html.*
[122] Reuters, "Opposition Leads Bain to Call Off 3Com Deal," March 21, 2008. *http://www.nytimes.com/2008/03/21/technology/21com.html*.
[123] Bloomberg.com press release data/public filings/multiple press reports, September 28, 2007.
[124] Bloomberg.com, "3-Com Agrees to $2.2 billion dollar purchase," September 28, 2007.
125 Mobile Monday.Net, "UT Starcom Buys 3Com's Operator Assets,",March 5, 2003. Quote from the article: "Acquiring the CommWorks assets will allow UT Starcom to add to its base of tier-one customers and accelerate its geographic diversification outside of China," said Hong Lu, president and chief executive officer of UT Starcom. "We are already the largest vendor to China Telecom and sell to major customers such as China Netcom."

- 2007: 3Com sees the H3C venture as an option for reversing its multiyear unprofitable trend and decides to acquire and keep total ownership of H3C. Huawei sells 3Com its 49 percent share of the H3C joint venture.
- 2007: 3Com announces its acquisition by Bain Capital Partners and Huawei for $2.2 billion.
- 2008: 3Com acquisition by Bain and Huawei falls through due to regulatory opposition.[126]
- 2009: In November, 3Com announces acquisition by Hewlett-Packard for $2.7 billion.

Many industry analysts viewed the attempted acquisition of 3Com in concert with Bain as another example of Huawei's efforts to expand its products to overseas markets that it had not yet penetrated, as well as a way of competing directly against global leaders such as Cisco. Huawei was particularly interested in penetrating the North American marketplace at the enterprise solution level.[127]

DEALS IN THE TELECOM SECTOR, AND THE ROLE OF CFIUS

The Committee on Foreign Investment in the United States is a U.S. government interagency committee chaired by the Treasury Department. Its role is "to review transactions that could result in control of a U.S. business by a foreign person ('covered transactions'), in order to determine the effect of such transactions on the national security of the United States."[128] The CFIUS process is usually initiated when parties to a proposed or pending transaction of potential concern jointly file a voluntary notice with CFIUS. [129]

Membership in CFIUS includes the secretaries of seven federal departments (the Treasury, Justice, Homeland Security, Commerce, Defense, State, and Energy), and the heads of two executive offices (U.S. Trade Representative, Science & Technology Policy). The director of National Intelligence and the secretary of Labor are also nonvoting, ex officio members of CFIUS; and five additional federal offices (Office of Management & Budget, Council of Economic Advisors, National Security Council, National Economic Council, and Homeland Security Council) also participate as observer members of CFIUS.[130]

CFIUS investigates only a limited number of cases each year. It officially blocks only a very small number, although some deals are withdrawn by the filing companies if problems appear likely to crop up in the CFIUS review. In the three-year period from 2006 to 2008, CFIUS received a total of 404 notices (in all industrial sectors) and investigated 36 of them; 57 of these

[127] Reuters, "Opposition Leads Bain to Call Off 3Com Deal," March 21, 2008. http://www.nytimes.com/2008/03/21/technology/21com.html; and *Caijing China* (English version), "The 3Com Deal, Behind the Security Flap," October 23, 2007.

[127] Funding Universe.com/histories; 10Ks, public filings.

[128] United States Department of the Treasury website, "Office of Investment Security -- Committee on Foreign Investment in the United States." http://www.ustreas.gov/offices/international-affairs/cfius. CFIUS operates pursuant to section 721 of the Defense Production Act of 1950, as amended by the Foreign Investment and National Security Act of 2007 (section 721) and as implemented by Executive Order 11858, as amended, and regulations at 31 C.F.R. Part 800.

[129] United States Department of the Treasury website, "Office of Investment Security -- Committee on Foreign Investment in the United States – Overview of the CFIUS Process." http://www.ustreas.gov/offices/international-affairs/cfius/overview.shtml.

[130] United States Department of the Treasury website, "Office of Investment Security -- Committee on Foreign Investment in the United States – Composition of CFIUS." http://www.ustreas.gov/offices/international-affairs/cfius/members.shtml.

proposed deals were subsequently withdrawn after filing, but none were formally rejected.[131] In the same period, CFIUS reviewed a total of 133 cases classified as "information" sector deals (one-third of the total number); of these, 22 cases were in the telecommunications industry.[132] Three out of the total 133 "information sector" deals involved investors based in China.[133]

Huawei, in particular, has been a focus of great attention and controversy in association with CFIUS reviews of potential telecom deals. As stated by the *Financial Times:*

> *US government agencies charged with reviewing sensitive acquisitions are engaged in a debate over how to handle Huawei... There are two schools of thought within the US government. One pragmatic view holds that [CFIUS] should approve a future transaction [with Huawei] because it would allow the government to negotiate what is known as a mitigation agreement, a set of strict conditions and security-related requirements that could give the US valuable insight into the inner workings of a company that some allege has close ties to the Chinese military...*

> *But there are strong arguments against such a move that support keeping Huawei at bay. One former official close to the [CFIUS] process said the government engaged in a similar debate during its review of Huawei's joint bid for 3Com... 'At the time, most of the national security agencies concluded that the window into Huawei would not be useful enough and that it would be very difficult to write procedures that would ensure [network security]...'[134]*

CFIUS and the Abortive Emcore / Caofeidian Deal

Aside from the abortive deal between Huawei and 3Com, another recent Chinese-related telecommunication deal that encountered difficulties with CFIUS was the cancelled 2010 deal between Emcore Corporation and China's Tangshan Caofeidian Investment Corporation [*Tangshan Caofeidian Touzi Jituan* / 唐山曹妃甸投资集团], or TCIC. Emcore Corporation, a New Mexico-based manufacturer of components for fiber optic equipment and solar panels, had agreed to sell a 60 percent stake in its fiber optics business to TCIC for $27.75 million USD.[135]

There is little known about TCIC; the company has no website, and only limited information regarding the investment firm is readily available. It is possible that TCIC is a subsidiary of the Tangshan Caofeidian Infrastructure Investment Corporation [*Tangshan Caofeidian Jichu Sheshi Jianshe Touzi Jituan Youxian Gongsi* / 唐山曹妃甸基础设施建设投资集团有限公司], a state-owned conglomerate created by the Caofeidian Ministry of Investment. The company is a key

---

[131] Committee on Foreign Investment in the United States, *Annual Report to Congress 2009* (Washington, DC: November 2009), p. 3. *http://www.ustreas.gov/offices/international-affairs/cfius/docs/2009%20CFIUS%20Annual%20Report.pdf.*

[132] Committee on Foreign Investment in the United States, *Annual Report to Congress 2009* (Washington, DC: November 2009), pp. 4 and 7. *http://www.ustreas.gov/offices/international-affairs/cfius/docs/2009%20CFIUS%20Annual%20Report.pdf.*

[133] Committee on Foreign Investment in the United States, *Annual Report to Congress 2009* (Washington, DC: November 2009), p. 15. *http://www.ustreas.gov/offices/international-affairs/cfius/docs/2009%20CFIUS%20Annual%20Report.pdf.*

[134] Stephanie Kirchgaessner and Helen Thomas, "US Divided on How to Tackle Huawei," *Financial Times,* July 29, 2010.

[135] Emcore Corp. Press Release, "EMCORE and Tangshan Caofeidian Investment Corporation ('TCIC') Pursue Alternative Means of Cooperation to Address Regulatory Concerns," June 28, 2010. *http://www.emcore.com/news_events/release?y=2010&news=249.*

player in the financial and economic development of Caofeidian, an industrial zone on a man-made island in the Gulf of Bohai. The Caofeidian project was initiated at the direction of the PRC State Council in 2004 and is administered by Tangshan City, Hebei Province.[136]

Tangshan Caofeidian Infrastructure Investment Corporation claims 28 subsidiaries and several equity affiliates. These subsidiaries and affiliates are reportedly involved in a wide variety of industries, to include real estate, hotels, railroads, logistical services, construction, petrochemicals, and even electric vehicle development.[137]

Figure 2: Location of Caofeidian Island

Source: *http://www.caofeidian.us/index.html.*

Figure 3: Artist Conception of Caofeidian Island

Source: *http://hy.csm.org.cn/icsr10/en/110.htm.*

Although it is unconfirmed, the TCIC involved in the Emcore deal may be associated with Tangshan Caofeidian Financial Investment, Ltd., [*Tangshan Caofeidian Touzi Youxian Zeren Gongsi* 唐山曹妃甸投资有限责任公司], a state-owned investment bank based in Caofeidian. The bank is involved in private equity investment, direct investment, consulting, and financial advisory services.[138] Tangshan Caofeidian Investment, Ltd., has invested in a plethora of domestic and foreign firms and funds, to include the China-Africa Development Fund, the China-Belgium Equity Investment Fund, the Bohai Industry Investment Fund, the China-ASEAN Investment Fund, China Aluminum Corporation, Mandarin Capital Partners [*Zhong-Yi Mandalin Jijin* / 中意曼达林基金, a joint investment project between Chinese and Italian banks],[139] as well as other "major projects that are in the interest of shareholders."[140]

---

[136] Caofeidian promotional website. *http://www.caofeidian.us/index.html.*

[137] "Tangshan Caofeidian Infrastructure Construction Dynamic Management Platform" [Tangshan Caofeidian Jichu Sheshi Jianshe Dongtai Guanli Pingtai / 唐山曹妃甸基础设施建设动态管理平台], "Company Introduction." Translation by USCC staff. *http://www.cfdjt.com/Integration/ProjectIntro.aspx.*

[138] *Daily Economic News* [*Mei Ri Jingji Xinwen* / 每日经济新闻], "National Development Bank Goes Through Tangshan Caofeidian to March into City Development" [*Guojia Kaifa Yinhang Jiedao Tangshan Caofeidian Zhijie Jinjun Chengshi Kaifa* / 国家开发银行借道唐山曹妃甸直接进军城市开发], March 10, 2010. Translation by USCC staff. *http://finance.ce.cn/rolling/201003/10/t20100310_15590232.shtml.*

[139] Mandarin Capital Partners website. *http://www.mandarincp.com/index.html.*

[140] *Daily Economic News* [*Mei Ri Jingji Xinwen* / 每日经济新闻], "National Development Bank Goes Through Tangshan Caofeidian to March into City Development" [*Guojia Kaifa Yinhang Jiedao Tangshan Caofeidian Zhijie Jinjun Chengshi Kaifa* / 国家开发银行借道唐山曹妃甸直接进军城市开发], March 10, 2010. Translation by USCC staff. *http://finance.ce.cn/rolling/201003/10/t20100310_15590232.shtml.*

The proposed deal between Emcore and TCIC was withdrawn in late June 2010.[141] As is its usual practice, CFIUS has not made any public statement about the matter. Emcore has stated only that CFIUS communicated "certain regulatory concerns about the transaction" and that "EMCORE and TCIC remain willing to explore alternative means of cooperation that would address regulatory concerns and meet the parties' objectives."[142]

THE GROWTH STRATEGY OF CHINESE TELECOM FIRMS

An apparent strategy for Chinese companies has been to pursue developing markets first and then move on to developed markets, as seen in the involvement of Chinese companies in telecom infrastructure markets in the 1980s and 1990s.[143] Their product strategy was to provide broad-scale telecommunications and network products for low procurement and implementation costs.[144]

Within China's domestic market, the government appears to have strongly favored domestically produced telecommunications products and services.[145] This protected environment allowed domestic firms such as Huawei and ZTE to gain strength and size while also being able to compete against world-class solutions providers such as Cisco, 3Com, Avaya, Nortel, Alcatel-Lucent, Ericsson, IBM, and others across a wide range of solution sets that may have been unsustainable in the face of free and open competition.

Huawei's initial forays into the global marketplace were into other Asian nations in China's economic near abroad.[146] This was the initial arena where some Chinese companies may have refined their strategy of "developing markets first, developed markets second" before moving forward with a strategy for global competition.[147]

Huawei has competed very successfully worldwide and is often in the number one or two slot in developing markets.[148] Its aggressive strategy and pricing have a major economic impact for both large and small service providers, and its market prospects appear positive. Nevertheless, if a company wants to ascend to the top tier of global telecommunications and networking equipment companies, historically it has been essential that it gain access to the U.S. marketplace. The North American market appears to have been one of Huawei's last target markets, as penetrating the U.S. marketplace promised to pose one of the toughest challenges and could remain a weaker market for Huawei for some time.[149] This may have driven much of

---

[141] Stephanie Kirchgaessner, "US Blocks China Fibre Optics Deal Over National Security," *Financial Times*, June 30, 2010; and Emcore Corp. Press Release, "EMCORE and Tangshan Caofeidian Investment Corporation ('TCIC') Pursue Alternative Means of Cooperation to Address Regulatory Concerns," June 28, 2010. *http://www.emcore.com/news_events/release?y=2010&news=249.*

[142] Emcore Corp. Press Release, "EMCORE and Tangshan Caofeidian Investment Corporation ('TCIC') Pursue Alternative Means of Cooperation to Address Regulatory Concerns," June 28, 2010. *http://www.emcore.com/news_events/release?y=2010&news=249*

[143] NPR.org, "Chinese Telecom Companies Look to Global Markets," August 16, 2005.

[144] Voice & Data Online, India, "ZTE Right Pricing," September 3, 2008.

[145] *Asia Times,* "3G is Key to a Foreign Telecom Role in China," December 6ʹ, 2006, and " Voice & Data Online, India, "ZTE Right Pricing," September 3, 2008.

[146] Voice & Data Online, India, "ZTE Right Pricing," September 3, 2008.

[147] RCR Wireless, "Huawei's Aggressive Push Pays Off," September 24, 2008.

[148] Del Oro Group Press Release, "Chinese Vendors Huawei and ZTE Gain Ground on Leaders Ericsson and Nokia Siemens," April 26, 2008.

[149] *Forbes*, "Huawei's U.S. coming out Party," March 27, 2009; and *Forbes*, "Huawei Buys Back Into 3Com," October 1, 2007.

Huawei's joint venture strategy with 3Com, which may be considered the company's first large, strategic attempt to move into U.S. markets.

The abortive deal with 3Com would have offered Huawei an opportunity to establish the beachhead for a stronger presence in the North American marketplace. It was also an opportunity for Huawei to jump on the mergers and acquisitions (M&A) bandwagon that was gaining momentum in the telecommunications industry. Huawei's statements indicated a desire to use its H3C joint venture with 3Com as a means of refining the focus of its product strategy to telecommunications service providers. However, its actions may have also indicated a more ambitious strategy for the North American market.[150] After 3Com bought out the H3C venture, it appears that Huawei may have used the resulting cash to turn back around and pursue 3Com in acquisition mode. Although its efforts in this regard were opposed by regulators *(see pp. 28-30),* this still serves as a useful example of the way in which Huawei's direct market entry was attempted.

Huawei can be expected to learn both from experience and from studying other companies as it refines its global business model and presence. As it expands into new areas of business and employs new marketing strategies, Huawei can be expected to evolve continually in ways that will facilitate penetration into the United States and other target global markets. After sufficient globalization of its business model, Huawei may continue to move from being an equipment and solution manufacturer/provider to being a foundational shaper of markets. By no longer merely competing within market space boundaries, Huawei may overcome market models that compete with its own in order to redefine the way telecommunications and networking technologies are consumed and perhaps even redefine the market spaces by itself.

Investments take many more forms than simply financial investments or acquisitions. Chinese companies have made thoughtful investments in leading-edge financial practices, management talent, expertise, global engineering, R&D, and training facilities. Consistent with industry practices, many Chinese companies have successfully recruited executives from other major telecommunications companies for decades in an effort to conform to or drive best global management practices.[151] These companies apparently have gone to great efforts to manage, compensate, and retain top talent for expanding market share and achieving corporate earnings growth: for example, Huawei recently recruited a former Nortel executive to run its European operations.[152]

EXPANSION INTO DEVELOPING MARKETS

China has made its mark in wireless networking products. It is postured potentially to become the global leader in wireless networking worldwide as its networking products become part of infrastructure contributions to developing nations. Developing nations have certain advantages when acquiring technology and communications infrastructures, principally because they are not encumbered by legacy infrastructure. In many cases, they will not need to invest in ground-based infrastructure for telecommunications and can go straight to wireless networks.

---

[150] *Forbes,* "Nortel's China Syndrome," January 12, 2009.

[151] Kevin Maney,"The New Face of IBM" - "China's biggest IT brand wants to go global. So it bought the PC division - and the world-class management - of an American icon. Who says being 'oceans apart' is a bad thing?" Wired, July 2005. *http://www.wired.com/wired/archive/13.07/lenovo.html.*

[152] Cellular News, "Huawei Taps Former Nortel Exec to European Job," July 13, 2009.

Outside of China, Chinese telecom companies have been aggressive in purchasing networks in the developing world. This expansion into emerging markets may have been facilitated in part by western investments in China, which have freed Chinese capital to reach outward for acquisitions in other parts of the world.[153] However, the main driver behind these acquisitions appears to be the PRC's "going out" strategy, intended to encourage China's selected "national champions" to compete in international markets. In regions that may have been underserviced for telecommunications products and services, the lower-cost options offered by Chinese firms can be a natural fit.

U.S. corporate investments in China's telecom infrastructure and technical capabilities may be allowing Chinese companies to redirect a very large amount of their investment capital to purchase assets and networks in emerging markets – thereby effectively degrading U.S. competitive postures in these same growth markets when they find themselves competing directly against Chinese firms. In addition, as foreign firms increasingly have their technologies developed and manufactured in China, this provides unique insights to Chinese firms that they are able to use to improve their own products, a trend that will strengthen China's competitive position in both U.S. and global markets.

Recently, China has continued its acquisition approach to building market share in emerging markets.[154] For example, in 2006, China Mobile acquired Millicom International Cellular, which operated mobile telephone services in some of the world's least-developed regions, to include parts of Central America, South America, Africa, and the Asia-Pacific region.[155] As China Mobile expands successfully into emerging markets, other Chinese telecom providers such as Huawei and ZTE also seem likely to displace western suppliers. Developments of this nature can be increasingly negative for western wireless network equipment providers.[156]

Likewise, in February 2007, China Mobile acquired a 100 percent stake in Paktel and renamed the company China Mobile Pakistan. At that time, "[a]ccording to China Mobile Pakistan's COO [chief operating officer] Zafar Usmani, China Mobile had invested $1.66 billion USD in Pakistan, creating 41,700 job opportunities for the country."[157] Following up on this investment, in February 2009 China Mobile Pakistan announced an additional investment of $500 million to construct networks and infrastructures in Pakistan under its "Zong" brand.[158]

Other recent deals have continued the pattern of Chinese telecom expansion. In October 2008, China announced a planned investment of $50 million USD to develop telecommunications facilities in Guinea-Bissau's national post and telecom operator (PTO) Guinea Telecom,

---

[153] Jason Singer and Jason Dean, "China Mobile Nears $5.3 Billion Deal For Millicom; Beijing's Biggest Purchase Overseas Would Intensify Push Into Emerging Markets," *China Daily*, May 25, 2006. http://www.chinadaily.com.cn/world/2006-05/25/content_600127.htm.

[154] CNNMoney.com, "China's New Frontier, Chinese Telecom gear maker Huawei and ZTE have already conquered Africa and Asia. Next stop: Latin America.." June 23, 2009.

[155] Jason Singer and Jason Dean, "China Mobile Nears $5.3 Billion Deal For Millicom Beijing's Biggest Purchase Overseas Would Intensify Push Into Emerging Markets," *China Daily*, May 25, 2006. http://www.chinadaily.com.cn/world/2006-05/25/content_600127.htm.

[156] David Jackson, "China Mobile - Millicom Deal Threatens Ericsson, Nokia, Lucent, Motorola, QualComm," SeekingAlpha.com, May 25, 2006. http://seekingalpha.com/article/11224-china-mobile-millicom-deal-threatens-ericsson-nokia-lucent-motorola-qualcom.

[157] China Tech News, "Pakistan Welcomes More Chinese Telecom Investment," February 18, 2009. http://www.chinatechnews.com/2009/02/18/8855-pakistan-welcomes-more-chinese-telecom-investment.

[158] China Tech News, "Pakistan Welcomes More Chinese Telecom Investment," February 18, 2009. http://www.chinatechnews.com/2009/02/18/8855-pakistan-welcomes-more-chinese-telecom-investment.

including the installation of a fiber-optic network to span the entire country, from the border with Senegal in the north to Guinea in the south.[159] Chinese telecoms are also reaching into wealthier nonwestern markets. In April 2009, China Mobile announced its desire to pursue an investment in the Taiwanese telecommunications company Far EasTone.[160] Instead, China Mobile gained approval to set up a subsidiary under its "Zong" brand, which will be used to source telecommunications handsets and equipment.[161]

A clear model has emerged: Chinese companies leverage their inexpensive and plentiful engineers, designers, contractors, and any others needed to build new networks or to upgrade existing networks in these emerging markets.[162] As western markets become saturated, these emerging markets become the growth areas and enable government-influenced telecommunication companies to find attractive new areas for expansion.[163] Where fixed-line infrastructure is poor or limited, cellular networks are much cheaper to roll out and are used as the primary means of communication."[164] As China expands its network influence and infuses its supply chains with propriety standards and equipment, China builds its global influence in the overall standards processes and becomes a much stronger player in developing global standards. By influencing these global standards, China may increase the overall value of its own proprietary intellectual property.

THE EAST-WEST FLOW OF INVESTMENTS IN THE COMMUNICATIONS SECTOR

> Investments between China and the United States have become symbiotic, with results that may not have been immediately apparent at the outset. Chinese and American companies have shared in both the risks and the rewards in their capitalist ventures.[165] While the events cataloged in this report lead to the eventual conclusion that American network security could *potentially* be imperiled, our national security also depends upon how we manage our business relationships with China and how we deal with the successive companies that have been born out of our broad trading framework. National security will not be effectively maintained without economic security.

Through the use of mergers and acquisitions, the aggressive application of sovereign wealth funds, joint ventures, and many other business mechanisms, China is rapidly gaining the

---

[160] PriMetrica, Inc.,"Guinea Telecom to receive USD50m in Chinese investment" (Carlsbad, CA: October 21, 2008. http://www.telegeography.com/cu/article.php?article_id=25675.

[161] Dow Jones & Company, Inc., "Taiwan stocks on fire on China Mobile-Far EasTone.Deal Plan," *Wall Street Journal* Digital Network, MarketWatch, Inc. Asia Markets, April 29, 2009. http://www.marketwatch.com/story/china-mobiles-taiwan-plan-could-change-everything.

[161] Chinmei Sung and Janet Ong, "Taiwan Opens 100 Industries to Chinese Investment (Update2)," Bloomberg, June 30, 2009. http://www.bloomberg.com/apps/news?pid=20601080&sid=aFeN1SK55G7U; and NetworkWorld, "China Mobile Wins Approval for Taiwan Subsidiary," May 11, 2010.

[162] Jason Singer and Jason Dean, "China Mobile Nears $5.3 Billion Deal For Millicom Beijing's Biggest Purchase Overseas Would Intensify Push Into Emerging Markets," China Daily Information Co. (CDIC), May 25, 2006. http://www.chinadaily.com.cn/world/2006-05/25/content_600127.htm.

[163] Jason Singer and Jason Dean "China Mobile Nears $5.3 Billion Deal For Millicom Beijing's Biggest Purchase Overseas Would Intensify Push Into Emerging Markets'" China Daily Information Co. (CDIC), May 25, 2006. http://www.chinadaily.com.cn/world/2006-05/25/content_600127.htm; and Reuters, "Russia's MTS (WHAT IS MTS?) picks Huawei for 3G Armenia Network," January 16, 2009.

[164] Jason Singer and Jason Dean "China Mobile Nears $5.3 Billion Deal For Millicom Beijing's Biggest Purchase Overseas Would Intensify Push Into Emerging Markets," China Daily Information Co. (CDIC), May 25, 2006. http://www.chinadaily.com.cn/world/2006-05/25/content_600127.htm.

[165] *Wall Street Journal* ,"China Ready to Place Bets on Hedge Funds," June 19, 2009.

potential for establishing global dominance in the telecommunications sector. Significant investments have been made in the communications sector over the last two decades, with substantial escalation occurring over the last ten years and increasing escalation over the most recent five years. These investments parallel the overall growth of Chinese investments in the United States and U.S. investments in China.

Some U.S. venture funds and hedge funds have targeted China exclusively in an effort to generate both growth and higher yields in their portfolios and to take advantage of China's burgeoning infrastructure build-out.[166] Many major venture capital and private equity firms have looked toward China for growth. Billions of dollars from firms such as Draper Fisher, Sycamore Ventures, The Carlyle Group Asia, Intel Capital (the venture arm of Intel), Softbank Asia, JP Morgan Asia – all firms with strong U.S. roots or investment ties – have been invested in Chinese telecommunications ventures since the early 2000s. Many of these companies are now publicly traded on exchanges like the NASDAQ, NYSE, FTSE, and NIKKEI.[167]

China has announced continued network investment at home on next-generation wireless technologies, potentially reaching 280 billion RMB (~$44B USD) in 2009.[168] Faced by an ongoing financial crisis in the United States, some U.S. venture firms have announced a renewed investment strategy in China's infrastructure.[169] Networks of investment, venture capital, hedge funds, other financial instruments, and management entities seem almost as interconnected today as the technologies themselves.

China has also moved forward aggressively on an array of European partnerships that allow rapid growth in space-based communications markets.[170] This is due to the fact that companies from China are not only investors in foreign firms but are also investors in China's own "home-grown" manufacturing talent and capabilities base. Chinese companies have used mergers, acquisitions, and international partnerships to steadily and rapidly increase China's home-grown technologies – which, in many cases, might be more accurately identified as "grafted foreign hybrids."

Chinese companies have also made considerable investments through sovereign wealth funds in numerous hedge funds and investment banks. For example, Beijing Wonderful Investments/The China Investment Corporation recently took an expanded 12.5 percent stake in Blackstone Group.[171] Blackstone's private equity group has, over the years, taken stakes in companies like T-Mobile (one of the largest wireless cellular carriers in the global market, including the United States), TDC Telecom, Sungard (provider of backup, disaster recovery, and storage solutions – provider of critical disaster recovery services to the U.S. government), Global Tower (an operator of towers for wireless networks), NewSkies (a broadband satellite communications company), TRW Automotive, Charter Communications, Adelphia Communications (cable), iPCS (wireless communications provider), and StorageApps (provider of storage area networking solutions).[172]

---

[166] *New York Times*, "Silverlake Eyes Asia Tech Investments," November 28, 2008.
[167] Asia Private Equity Review, April 2006; China C SR [corporate social responsibility], May 27, 2008.
[168] *China Daily*, "China Finally Awards Telecom Operators 3G Wireless," January 7, 2009.
[169] Annual Reports and 10K filings, Carlyle Group website. *www.carlyle.com.*
[170] Alcatel Alenia Press Release, "Alcatel Alenia Space Wins New Communication and Broadcast Satellite Contract Chinasat 6B From ChinaSatcom, Bolstering Cooperation With China," redOrbit.com, December 5, 2005.
[171] Blackstone 10K Filing 2009. Annual Report and consolidated financial statements.
[172] The Blackstone Group. *http://www.blackstonegroup.com.*

Patterns of these investments suggest the potential for a continual increase of Chinese investments in global business markets, which might also provide deep access by PRC government-influenced or controlled actors to both influential foreign companies and to sensitive communications networks. However, as with any investment, it is also possible that investments and relationships such as these continually will open doors to new opportunities to expand business lines and portfolios constructively. Many American businesses have embraced strong ties with Asian companies over the last few decades, and the American consumer less frequently associates negative brand identity with Chinese technology products, particularly when they are paired with major American, Japanese, or European brand identities.

SECTION 2
POTENTIAL VULNERABILITIES IN COMMUNICATIONS INFRASTRUCTURE AND PRODUCTS, AND CHINESE INVESTMENTS IN THESE SECTORS

Note: This report mentions only a few actors and fields of technology, representing a fraction of the various actors, technologies, and relationships present in the communications sector. They were selected because references are often more readily available or particularly noteworthy. Although valid examples, they may not be fully representative of the overall sector environments themselves.

Efforts to analyze potential technological risks are often plagued by a failure to account for the continuous nature of technological innovation, difficulties associated with "control dilemmas,"[173] and faulty assumptions of a continuity of currently prevailing trends. New technologies are constantly evolving, and U.S. technological competitiveness will be challenged frequently in the future and from many quarters. As applies to this analysis, U.S. policymakers and industry officials cannot fully understand and appreciate the risks of China's rising influence in the communications sector until that influence has become somewhat manifest. Nevertheless, working continually toward reasonable forecasts of risks is necessary in light of the potential national security stakes involved.

INVESTMENTS IN LONG-HAUL FIBER

Fiber is being used extensively worldwide as the primary means of high-bandwidth communication, to include advanced digital video and data and high-speed Internet and telephony applications. In the past few years, the number of new fiber connections has outpaced the number of new copper cable connections, principally due to the superior performance of fiber technology.[174] Fiber has become the transport technology of choice because it has thousands of times the bandwidth of copper wire and can carry signals hundreds of times farther before needing a repeater. Most carrier-level or business network backbones are fiber-based using Ethernet standards.[175]

Insofar as sensitive U.S. data are transported across global undersea networks, the data are vulnerable to interception or interference by hostile actors but perhaps only by degrees more so than before. Hacking into optical networks is not overly difficult. Perhaps the easiest and consequently most undetectable means is simply bending a cable, as this will allow a small (but sufficient amount) of light to leak from the cable without actually breaking connections – something that operations engineers try to be very quick to notice and investigate. A "tap" is completed by using commercially available couplers to place a microbend in the cable to allow light to radiate through the cladding and be exposed to a photodetector. The photodetector is connected to an electro-optical converter that acts as an interface to a network interface card. This tap allows the data being transmitted through the cable to be intercepted and "sniffed" for

---

[173] A "control dilemma" relates to the fact that the catastrophic risks of new changes and technologies often cannot be known until they have been implemented to the degree necessary for the risks to be incurred.
[174] InfoTech News, "Research and Markets: Gigabit Ethernet Fiber and Copper Cabling Systems," TMCNET.com, April 15, 2010.
[175] Cisco website. *http://www.cisco.com/en/US/docs/internetworking/technology/handbook/Ethernet.pdf*.

desired information in much the same way as any network data may be compromised.[176] Splicing is another method for tapping fiber optic cables but is much more difficult to perform successfully, as it usually results in briefly breaking the connection, which may lead to detection. When millions of connections are severed, even momentarily, this is noteworthy and will possibly lead to an investigation of the event by affected carriers.[177]

The potential for disruption of communications through undersea cables was seen in December 2006 when an earthquake broke cables in the South China Sea between Taiwan and the Philippines, disabling 90 percent of the region's telecommunications capacity. It was demonstrated again in January and February 2008 when cables in Middle Eastern waters were reportedly broken by stray ship anchors. The cable outages disrupted a wide variety of communications, to include the ability of the U.S. military's Central Command to communicate with facilities and units in Iraq and Afghanistan.[178]

Whether fiber is cut by accident, by design to disrupt communications, or hacked to intercept sensitive data, the threat to national security can be significant. All fiber networks consist of complex electronic components, many of which are manufactured outside of the United States. These components could form another source of insecurity, as they can be infected with malicious code such as kill switches, Trojan horses, worms, or many other harmful features during the manufacture process. Repair parts[179] and diagnostic tools also can be a source of malware exposing fiber communications to third-party eavesdropping. The United States has placed itself in a position of relying on other countries for much of its technology infrastructure, a set of circumstances with serious implications for network security. (For more on this subject, see sec. 3 of this report, "Supply Chain Integrity, and the Impact on Government/Defense Contracting.")

The Security of Optical Fiber Networks, and the Case of Global Crossing and Hutchison-Whampoa

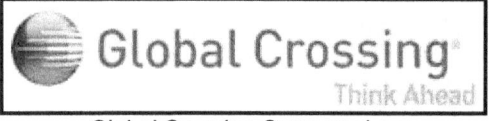

Global Crossing Company Logo
Source: Global Crossing.com.

Hutchison Whampoa Company Logo
Source: Hutchison-Whampoa.com.

In late 1999, an aggressive global fiber optic build-out was in progress as the Internet boom pushed the development of optical fiber networks to carry greater traffic loads at increasing speeds. This spurred increased construction of an undersea fiber to bridge high-density points in Asia and Europe. Global Crossing, a holding company based in Bermuda with significant U.S. and global interests, made significant investments in high-capacity undersea fiber routes, ultimately establishing a "$20 billion global fiber optic network [that] crosses both the Atlantic and Pacific Oceans and connects twenty-seven countries in Asia, North and South America and

---

[176] Sandra Kay Miller, "Hacking at the Speed of Light," SecuritySolutions.com, April 1, 2006.
[177] Sandra Kay Miller, "Hacking at the Speed of Light," SecuritySolutions.com, April 1, 2006. http://securitysolutions.com/mag/security_hacking_speed_light.
[178] James Geary, "Who Protects the Internet?" Popular Science, March 13, 2009.
[179] Reperi - Integrated circuits (ICs) can be altered to introduce malware into the hardware. That includes replacement parts that consist of ICs. Specifically, fiber uses transceivers and multiplexers along with other equipment. Any of these devices can be sources of malware.

Europe."[180] Global Crossing's interests have been strategically significant because of the depth of its holdings in undersea cable connecting key strategic transport routes and its exposure to U.S. government communications traffic through substantial holdings and the holdings of subsidiaries.

Figure 4: Global Crossing Networks in 2010

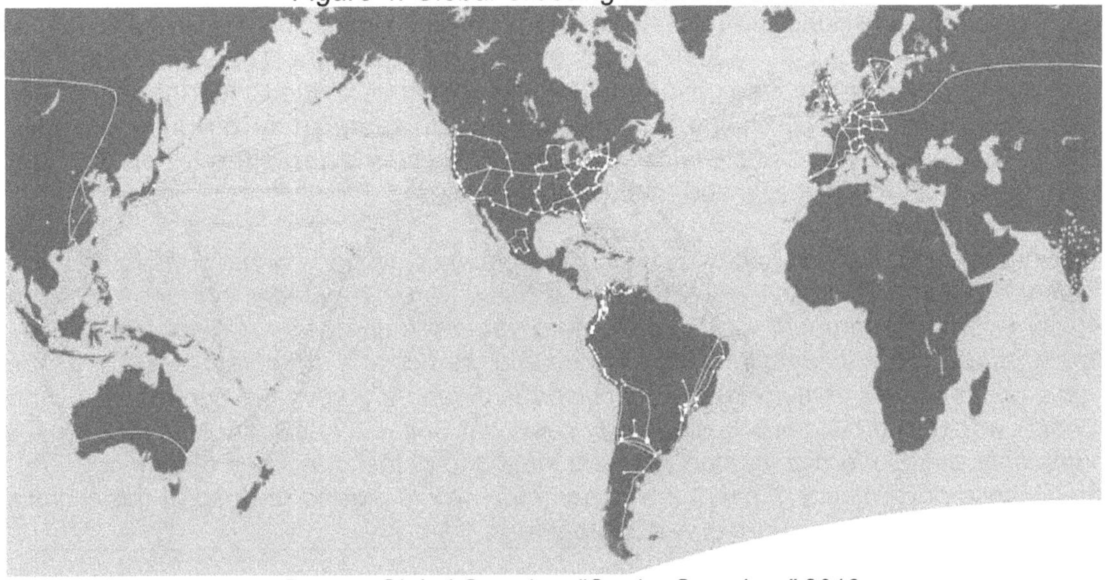

Source: Global Crossing, "Carrier Overview," 2010.

Overestimating demand and timing caused a telecommunications bust cycle in the early 2000s, resulting in bankruptcy filings by long-haul fiber carriers. Hutchison Whampoa had a $400 million convertible bond stake in Global Crossing at the time Global Crossing entered bankruptcy in 2002. In early 2002, Singapore Telecom (ST Telemedia) and Hutchison Whampoa of Hong Kong attempted to acquire a majority stake in Global Crossing's network assets at a price of $750 million).[181] Hutchison Whampoa subsequently withdrew from the purchase agreement and ST Telemedia exercised its option under the purchase agreement to assume all of Hutchison's rights and obligations, purchasing a 61.5 percent stake in Global Crossing (reorganized following bankruptcy) for $250 million.[182] These actions were taken due to ongoing CFIUS objections to the potential role of Hutchison Whampoa.[183] *(For more on telecom deals that ran afoul of CFIUS, see pp. 30-33.)*

Hutchinson Whampoa is Hong Kong's largest multinational conglomerate, operating in 54 countries worldwide. The company holds a broad range of investments, from health and beauty products to port operations, property development, and telecommunications.[184] To date, Hutchison Whampoa is the largest company traded on the Hong Kong Stock Exchange, with a

---

[180] James Lewis, "CFIUS - The Committee on Foreign Investment in the United States" (Washington, DC: Center for Strategic and International Studies, February 2006). *http://csis.org/files/media/csis/pubs/060212_cfius.pdf.*

[181] Global Crossing Press Release, "Hutchison Whampoa Limited and Singapore Technologies Telemedia Pte. Ltd. Plan to Invest $750 Million in Global Crossing," January 8, 2002.

[182] Global Crossing Press Release, "ST Telemedia Increases Proposed Stake in Global Crossing," April 30, 2003; and Global Crossing 2003, 2004 10K SEC [Securities and Exchange Commission] filings.

[183] James Lewis, "New Objectives for CFIUS: Foreign Ownership, Critical Infrastructure, and Communications Interception," *Federal Communications Law Journal* (June 2005). *http://www.law.indiana.edu/fclj/pubs/v57/no3/Lewis.pdf.*

[184] Hutchison Whampoa Limited, About HWL. *http://www.hutchison-whampoa.com/eng/about/overview.htm.*

total market capitalization of HKD $205.7 billion.[185] The company was British owned until 1979, when Hong Kong and Shanghai Banking Corporation (HSBC) sold its controlling 22 percent stake to Cheung Kong Holdings, owned by Hong Kong tycoon Li Ka-Shing, for HKD $639 million.

Commonly referred to in Hong Kong as "Superman," Li Ka-Shing is the 11th richest man in the world, with a net worth of USD $23.1 billion, making him the richest man in Asia.[186] Mr. Li maintains close ties to the Chinese government. He is a director of the China International Trust and Investment Corporation (CITIC), a state investment arm operated by the China government, and also serves on several state advisory bodies.[187] According to James Lewis, a research fellow with the Center for Strategic and International Studies:

"The crux of the opposition to Hutchison was the company's alleged connections to the Chinese government. Senior Chinese government officials are reputedly among Hutchison's stockholders. The Department of Defense and others feared that China could use this investment relationship to influence Hutchison and particularly to obtain access to Global Crossing's communications networks… Hutchison is clearly a legitimate, commercial, publicly-traded entity with a long history of business success, but Chinese intelligence entities have used their ownership stake in foreign companies as a means to obtain controlled technology. The fear that the Chinese government, if given the opportunity, would extend the use of this technology to collect communications is not an unreasonable fear."[188]

ROUTERS, SWITCHES, AND HUBS

Routers are used to connect users between networks, while switches and hubs are used to connect users within a network. With advances in technology, many routers are now designed to perform the functions of switches and hubs as well as other security services such as intrusion detection/prevention and antivirus scanning. Routers have become the "Swiss army knife" of networking. Most networks are designed for redundancy and have multiple routers so that the failure of a few will not cause a complete network outage. In the case of an outage, routing tables of the remaining routers are reconfigured, and the network continues functioning, although at a reduced level until faulty routers can be repaired or replaced.

Typically, network customers subscribe with an Internet service provider (ISP) or carrier to transport their traffic between networks. When traffic is destined for a network using a different ISP as their carrier, some means must be provided to hand the traffic off to the other carrier for final delivery to the destination. Carriers may enter into their own teaming or peering

---

[185] *Bloomberg Businessweek*, HUTCHISON WHAMPOA LTD (13: Hong Kong).
http://investing.businessweek.com/research/stocks/snapshot/snapshot.asp?ticker=13:HK.
[186] Michael Schuman, "The Miracle of Asia's Richest Man," *Forbes,* February 24, 2010.
http://www.forbes.com/2010/02/24/li-ka-shing-billionaire-hong-kong-richest-opinions-book-excerpt-michael-schuman.html?boxes=Homepagelighttop.
[187] Stephen Vines, "The Other Handover," *TIMEasia*, August 6, 2005.
www.time.com/time/asia/2005/journey/hutchison.htm.
[188] James Lewis, "New Objectives for CFIUS: Foreign Ownership, Critical Infrastructure, and Communications Interception," *Federal Communications Law Journal* (June 2005).
http://www.law.indiana.edu/fclj/pubs/v57/no3/Lewis.pdf. Others have also voiced concerns about Hutchison Whampoa: for example, former Senate Majority Leader Trent Lott once went so far as to allege that Hutchison Whampoa is "an arm of the People's Liberation Army." See *Economist*, "Keeping Out Li Ka-Shing," May 3, 2003. However, a detailed examination of these allegations, or a deeper study of the background of Hutchison Whampoa, is beyond the scope of this report.

arrangements to handle such traffic or use an Internet exchange point (IXP) that has been set up for this specific purpose. An Internet exchange point is the physical infrastructure that allows ISPs to exchange Internet traffic between their networks by means of mutual peering arrangements that allow traffic to be exchanged without cost. These IXPs use a host of networking equipment, including sophisticated routers and switches to enable traffic to be properly routed.

This equipment is comprised of integrated circuits that can be severely impacted through malicious circuits that modify functionality or include backdoors and/or kill switches. Although a hostile actor manufacturing such products could conceivably target all integrated circuits to be used in routers, they might instead target integrated circuits used in the most sophisticated equipment, thus assuring the maximum amount of damage per individual attack. Following this line of reasoning, the Internet in the United States could theoretically be brought down or severely disrupted because the routers and switches serving the IXPs were disabled and traffic could no longer be routed between networks, except where carriers had their own private peering arrangements. Generally, the larger the network, the more sophisticated the equipment (such as routers and switches) becomes. Arguably, by focusing on the larger classes of routers and switches, a potential enemy could disrupt the most traffic and cause the greatest amount of harm with the fewest resources expended in an attack.[189]

However, this does not preclude strategies based on attacking large numbers of lower-end equipment components. Cyber attacks can be shaped in many different ways and attack the full spectrum of systems and networks. Depending on which effects are desired and tools that are available, cyber attackers may use old techniques to attack new systems effectively or may find that the massive effects of attacks based on using multitudes of smaller compromised components (workstations, access points, low-end routers, smart phones, etc.) can easily outweigh the effects of attacking higher-end systems or networks.

One of the central reasons that the proposed purchase of 3Com by Bain Capital and Huawei proved so controversial was the prominent position of 3Com in the router market. As a manufacturer of routers, switches, and hubs, 3Com had equipment that was often found in the heart of telecommunications networks and provided connectivity into some of the most secure areas of critical infrastructures. 3Com was also a significant provider of data communications equipment to the U.S. federal government.[190] *(For a fuller account of the abortive deal between 3Com and Huawei, see pp. 28-30.)* The U.S. companies Cisco and Juniper still hold a large share of the global high-end router market; however, Huawei is growing quickly and expanding worldwide, causing U.S. companies to lose ground.[191]

---

[189] Reperi – nonpublic research - there are numerous vectors for attacks intended to have a large-scale impact, and the possibility of massive attacks at large numbers of smaller routers is very real. However, some consider striking at large routers to be more attractive.

[190] Reuters, "Opposition Leads Bain to Call Off 3Com Deal," March 21, 2008. *http://www.nytimes.com/2008/03/21/technology/21com.html*; and *Cajing China (*English version), "The 3Com Deal, Behind the Security Flap," October 23, 2007.

[191] "Cisco and Juniper's combined market share fell from 69% in 2008 to 59% in 2009. Huawei and Alcatel-Lucent gained much of the share these companies lost." See TelecomsEurope.net, "Cisco, Juniper Lose Routing Market Share in 2009," February 22, 2010. *http://www.telecomseurope.net/content/cisco-juniper-lose-routing-market-share-2009.*

WiMAX/WiFi – NETWORK AND NETWORK CONTROL DEVICES AND PROTOCOLS FOR WIRELESS NETWORKING

Over the past decade, WiFi (wireless fidelity) has significantly raised the amount of interest in the wireless market. It is quickly becoming a replacement for or addition to wireline Ethernet in the business community and the access method of choice in the home. The creation of WiFi hot spots in locations such as airports, hotels, and coffee houses offers greater user mobility in connecting to service providers for data and voice transmissions. There are multiple standards in widespread use today, including 802.11a, 802.11b, 802.11g, and fairly recent developments such as 802.11n. The difference in each is in the frequency spectrum and modulation technology use, and the transmission rates available.

Worldwide Interoperability for Microwave Access (WiMAX) is a relatively new standard approved in January 2003 that will offer a last-mile alternative to digital subscriber line (DSL) and cable modem service, promising to lead to ubiquitous, continuous, mobile wireless connectivity. Huawei makes this type of equipment and will become a vendor to Clearwire Communications as the company rolls out 4G services at multiple locations in the United States. WiMAX can provide broadband on demand or last-mile wireless access to speed the deployment of IEEE 802.11 WiFi hotspots and wireless LANs. Public safety trials among various network providers in the United States have included utilizing WiMAX combined with Land Mobile Radio (LMR) applications to deliver public safety communications between multiple law enforcement and emergency responders. Clearwire has been quoted in the press regarding its intent to offer public safety solutions over its network.[192] Sprint Nextel is a major equity investor in Clearwire.[193]

Understanding China's internal domestic telecommunications market is essential to understanding Chinese communications investments in U.S. companies and around the world. China's own market for wireless communications has made it an attractive target for U.S. investment and an inexpensive development and manufacturing hub for wireless technologies. In the wireless world, it presents the mass market of mass markets, where manufacturing for wireless equipment can more easily cultivate economies of scale.

China began issuing 3G licenses for its internal spectrum in January 2009. The first three companies receiving licenses were China Mobile (TD-SCDMA - the domestically developed 3G standard), China Telecom (CDMA2000 - U.S. developed), and China Unicom (WCDMA - Europe developed).[194] The Chinese Ministry of Industry and Information Technology provided regulatory oversight for 3G network operation, dealing with competition, consumer rights, security, telecom charges management, and facilities.[195]

---

[192] WiMAX is a telecommunications technology providing wireless transmission of data using a variety of transmission modes, from point-to-multipoint links to portable and fully mobile Internet access. Based on the IEEE 802.16 standard (Broadband Wireless Access), WiMAX can be thought of as a more powerful relative of WiFi. For directional use, under ideal conditions WiMAX can reach between line-of-sight points for as far as 20 miles or more to connect local hotspots into a larger wireless wide-area network. Meanwhile, WiMAX hotspots can be as much as five or six miles across. A user may have a WiFi hotspot in their home that talks to a WiMAX hotspot in their neighborhood, which is connected to a WiMAX backbone that connects to the Internet at a distant location.
[193] Clearwire Press Release, May 7, 2008.
[194] *China Daily,* "China's telecom sector gets 3G licenses," January 7, 2009. http://www.chinadaily.com.cn/bizchina/2009-01/07/content_7375721.htm.
[195] *China Daily,* "China's telecoms sector gets 3G licenses," January 7, 2009. http://www.chinadaily.com.cn/bizchina/2009-01/07/content_7375721.htm.

At the same time, China has been making massive investments in 4G technology. The "Next-Generation Broadband Wireless Mobile Communications Network" began in 2008 and will stretch over 15 years, with total spending expected to reach 70 billion RMB (close to $10 billion USD).[196] China has been trying to promote its own standards for international adoption but has yet to achieve this goal. The network standard LTE is considered to be the next standard for replacing and upgrading 3G/4G systems and includes both frequency division and time division duplexes.[197] TeliaSonera, a Scandinavian telecom company, launched the first live LTE 4G services in Norway and Sweden in December 2009 using Huawei infrastructure in the Norway deployment. China Mobile launched the world's first TD (time division) LTE network recently providing download speeds ten times faster than 3G networks.[198] A significant number of LTE trials are already underway worldwide with Huawei having premier product entries in this market segment.

Huawei and the Development of LTE Standards[199]

Long-Term Evolution (LTE) is a "high performance air interface for cellular mobile telephony,"[200] and many of the world's leading telecommunications firms (including Verizon Wireless and AT&T) are working on potentially converting their networks to LTE technology.[201] The emergence of the LTE standard is the result of collaboration between telecommunications industry associations in Europe, Japan, China, South Korea, and North America. A number of international corporations are competing or collaborating in this market space, to include Cisco (United States), Ericsson (Sweden), Huawei (China), LG Technologies (Korea), Motorola (United States), Nokia Siemens Networks (Finland), Samsung (Japan), and ZTE (China).

Huawei has set for itself a strategic goal to become an industry leader in fixed wireline networks, wireless networks, and network switch segments worldwide. By spring of 2009, Huawei had become number two globally in the fixed wireline and network switch segment and number three in the wireless segment. Within the wireless segment, Huawei is investing considerable resources in the development of LTE technology.[202] Huawei has been involved with LTE research and development since 2004 and as of July 2010 had "been awarded 14 LTE commercial contracts and more than 60 LTE trials, including the world's first commercial LTE network in Oslo, Norway... [Huawei] intends to remain ahead of the industry curve by providing leading edge and customer-specific LTE solutions to allow operators around the world to establish and maintain long-term, competitive LTE leadership."[203]

Interlocutors speaking on behalf of Huawei have cited the company's superior position in LTE technology as a compelling reason for western telecom companies to adopt its products. Huawei's products are not necessarily superior to those of other suppliers worldwide: they are comparable in some ways and inferior or superior in others, depending on relative product development strategies. However, Huawei is competing fiercely in the entire LTE business model, to include services and management, and it might be able to position its product

---

[196] Kaiser Kuo, "China's 4G Master Plan," February 26, 2008. *http://digitalwatch.ogilvy.com.cn/en/?p=205*.

[197] Kaiser Kuo, "China's 4G Master Plan," February 26, 2008. *http://digitalwatch.ogilvy.com.cn/en/?p=205*.

[198] CNET News, "TeliaSonera Launches First LTE 4G Network," December 14, 2009; and Richard Wilson, "China Goes for 4G LTE in a Big Way," Electronicsweekly.com, July 29, 2009.

[199] The information in this section is based primarily on analysis provided to the Commission by Reperi LLC.

[200] See the entry for "LTE" in the glossary of this report, p. 97.

[201] Wireless Industry News, "AT and T Starts Building its LTE Network," February 11, 2010. *http://www.wirelessindustrynews.org/news-feb-2010/1836-021110-win-news.html.*

[202] Analysis provided to the Commission by Reperi LLC.

[203] Huawei website, "LTE Overview." *http://www.huawei.com/radio_access_network/lte.do.*

offerings to be less expensive than those of its competitors. U.S. telecommunications companies are under intense pressure to control costs, which may be forcing them to elevate pricing as a higher consideration than might otherwise have been the case.

The United States is currently faced by an accelerating technology paradigm shift in certain sectors, particularly telecommunications, in which foreign companies are moving into the position of being gatekeepers of standards in advanced technologies. Current-day decisions made by telecommunications companies regarding infrastructure build-outs will affect their business for years to come, and the question of which technology provider is likely to emerge as the industry leader is significant: "These telecom companies cannot afford (in a practical business sense) to choose a horse that won't win... *If* current trends continue... going with products from someone like Huawei might be viewed as a business survival decision, regardless of [any] potential security risks."[204]

APPLICATIONS SOFTWARE
Software/Controllers/Drivers

Networking equipment relies on controllers and/or drivers with associated software to deliver the functionality for which the equipment was designed. Since controllers may be embedded as integrated circuits in computer motherboards, routers, expansion cards, printer interfaces, or USB (universal serial bus) devices, they are subject to malicious actors inserting vulnerabilities that can render a device useless upon activation of a "kill" switch or changing the functionality in a way that reduces security by leaking or corrupting sensitive data. Controllers and drivers implemented through software are also potential sources of security vulnerabilities. Well-positioned actors with malicious intent can easily add viruses and other malware such as Trojans, worms, rootkits, spyware, and other malicious and unwanted software.

Applications software in wireless handsets, smart phones, and other network devices is one of the crucial components of overall wireless telecommunications solutions. TechFaith Wireless is a joint venture between Qualcomm and China's Techfaith to produce inexpensive software for wireless handsets.[205] Qualcomm is a manufacturer of wireless airlink technologies, chipsets, consumer electronics, hardware, mobile content services, secure phones, satellite phones (Globalstar), repeaters, wireless charging, and other devices.

NETWORK SECURITY PRODUCTS
Security Software

A trend is emerging of Chinese investment in network security companies and network security software and device manufacturing. In 2008, Huawei announced a joint venture with Symantec, a U.S. manufacturer of network security products best known for its popular antivirus software.[206] *(See text box on the following page.)* It is natural for communications manufacturers to gravitate to the network security space. However, as foreign companies gravitate to these parts of the supply chain, foreign network security products gain the potential

---

[204] Analysis provided to the Commission by Reperi LLC.

[205] AllBusiness.Com, "Qualcomm, China TechFaith Create Wireless Company," March 27, 2009.

[206]Symantec Press Release, "Huawei and Symantec Commence Joint Venture,", February 5, 2008. "...the company will develop and distribute world-leading security, and storage appliances to global telecommunications carriers and enterprises, and the transaction has satisfied all closing conditions received all required government and regulatory approvals..."

ability to be implemented in sensitive infrastructures unnoticed. China's technology manufacturers are increasingly moving into this security realm to meet their own growing needs, and their products therefore are appearing in global networks more frequently.

The Creation of Huawei Symantec

Huawei Symantec Company Logo

In February 2008, Huawei Technologies and the U.S.-based network security firm Symantec announced the creation of a joint venture to "develop and distribute world-leading security and storage appliances to global telecommunications carriers and enterprises." The resulting joint venture, "Huawei Symantec," was created with Huawei owning a 51 percent share of the company and Symantec owning a 49 percent share. John W. Thompson, chairman and chief executive officer of Symantec, serves as chairman of the board; Ren Zhengfei, chief executive officer of Huawei, serves as chief executive officer.

According to the company's website, it employs over 4,000 people and has expanded from its Chengdu headquarters into R&D centers in Chengdu, Beijing, Shenzhen, and Hangzhou. The company describes its mission as "combin[ing] Huawei's expertise in telecom network infrastructure and Symantec's leadership in security and storage software to provide world-class solutions" for network security and storage.[207]

The lack of transparency surrounding the operations and management of Huawei Technologies,[208] as well as the role of Symantec in designing and marketing network security products, could raise concerns in some quarters regarding potential national security issues associated with the joint venture. However, no specific allegations have been made against the company, and it has emerged as a significant competitor in the network security field.[209]

An important consideration in the market space for network security products is "technology refresh." If network protocols advance beyond the technical capabilities of security hardware, there are dangers of networks having traffic that is unmonitored passing through security zones undetected. An example would be IPv6 packets being tunneled through an IPv4 capable-only firewall. Theoretically, some elements of the IPv6 traffic could breach security without notice.[210]

Protecting telecommunications networks and the equipment and data that comprise these networks is essential to national security. Protection may be in the form of antivirus software

---

[207] Huawei Symantec website, "About Huawei Symantec." *http://www.huaweisymantec.com/en/About_Us/Company_Information/Company_Introduction.*

[208] See discussion of Huawei's management structure on page 15 of this report. See also Kevin O'Brien, "Upstart Chinese Telecom Company Rattles Industry as It Rises to No. 2," *New York Times,* November 29, 2009; and Kevin Eagles, "Huawei Needs To Be More Open on Security If It Is To Become a Global Player," *SC Magazine (UK),* November 6, 2009.

[210] For a list of the company's products and services, see Huawei Symantec website, "Products & Solutions." *http://www.huaweisymantec.com/en/Product___Solution.*

[210] Network World, "Invisible IPv6 Traffic Poses Serious Network Threat," July 13, 2009.

and the hardware/software comprising the various security appliances discussed above. Computer security is enhanced through the use of three processes: prevention, detection, and response. A failure in any of these processes could leave systems open to intrusion, with serious consequences. In the current environment of technology outsourcing, the opportunities for hostile nations to compromise U.S. security through the manipulation of security software or hardware used in critical infrastructure has increased dramatically. Reacting only when the threat materializes may prove to be far too late. The selection of sources for network security software and hardware begs careful consideration.

HANDSETS AND SMART PHONES

As the manufacture of mobile phone handsets and associated software moves to offshore outsourcers along with other technology equipment, security potentially could be compromised by actors with hostile intentions, thereby placing at risk one of the most widely used forms of communications in the United States.

Both of China's two largest telecom equipment companies, ZTE and Huawei, are amassing significant market share in the handset sector. Many of these handsets are made to work with 4G technologies (next-generation wireless). The Asian market has been an early adopter of standards that would allow 4G wireless technologies to expand rapidly; having the ability to roam freely across many types of networks is an essential element of handset compatibility. Many developing nations in South America, Africa, and Europe have followed suit.[211]

Huawei and ZTE's product lines compete with Motorola, Ericsson, LG, Samsung, and Apple. As markets shift, competition forces market participants to change relationships in order to adapt to new or emerging conditions. Most of these companies have agreements with one another to work together and develop certain product applications in order to stay competitive. According to press reports, Huawei and ZTE have been focused on developing, manufacturing, and selling technologically savvy, lower-cost products as Huawei moves to occupy market niches. [212] Both Huawei and ZTE have typically introduced their mobile phones into the United States and other markets through relabeling for companies like Verizon Wireless and T-Mobile. Huawei's new Android smart phone, manufactured for T-mobile, is a touch screen and Android-powered hand set. (The Android operating system and application technology model was initially developed by Google and then shifted to an open source alliance.) Android has an open software standard that moves easily between networks and protocols and features Google search, utilities, and applications capabilities. These features make the Huawei Android phone a competitive new entrant into the U.S. wireless market.

Figure 5: A T-Mobile UK "Pulse" Smartphone with Huawei Android Technology

---

[211]Firoze Manji and Stephen Marks, "African Perspectives on China in Africa," Fahamu--Network for Social Justice, 2007.
[212] CNNMoney.com, "China's New Frontier," June 25, 2009.

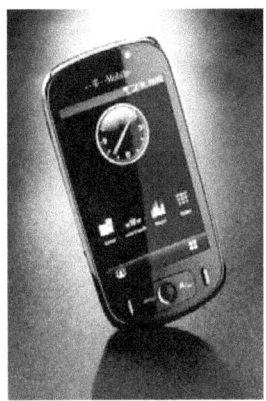
Source: Google Images.

There were some indications in early 2010 that the computer firm Lenovo might be taking steps to consider further acquisitions in the North American market. Speculation also appeared in the business press in spring 2010 that Lenovo might make a bid for Palm, with an eye toward getting into the smartphone market.[213] However, no confirmed action has occurred on such a deal as of the writing of this report. *(For further discussion of the controversy surrounding the sales of Lenovo equipment to the U.S. government, see pp. 66-68 of this report.)*

HANDSETS AND SMART PHONES: POTENTIAL VULNERABILITIES

How telephones/handsets are attacked is a useful study for understanding the vulnerabilities of communications equipment to malicious activity. From botnets[214] to SMiShing (SMS phishing) to battery draining,[215] the wireless handset is one of the latest and most favored vectors for

---

213 Kit Eaton, "Lenovo Wants in on Smartphone Biz, Acquiring Palm Could be the Ticket," *Fast Company,* April 19, 2010. *http://www.fastcompany.com/1620623/lenovo-mobile-internet-smartphones-finances-growth-palm-palm-os-pre-pixi?#.*

214 Fox News Network LLC, "Experts: Zombie Cell-Phone Hack Attacks May Be Next," October 16, 2008. *http://www.foxnews.com/story/0,2933,438481,00.html* : "[S]ome of the most vicious Internet predators are hackers who infect thousands of PCs [personal computers] with special viruses and lash the machines together into 'botnets' to pump out spam or attack other computers. Now security researchers say cell phones, and not just PCs, are the next likely conscripts into the automated armies. The mobile phone as zombie computer is one possibility envisioned by security researchers from Georgia Tech in a new report coming out Wednesday. The report identifies the growing power of cell phones to open a new avenue of attack for hackers. Of particular concern is that as cell phones get more computing power and better Internet connections, hackers can capitalize on vulnerabilities in mobile-phone operating systems or web applications. Botnets, or networks of infected or robot PCs, are the weapons of choice when it comes to spam and so-called 'denial of service attacks,' in which computer servers are overwhelmed with Internet traffic to shut them down."

215 ScienceDaily LLC, "Stealth Attack Drains Cell Phone Batteries," August 30, 2006: "Cell phones that can send or receive multimedia files could be targeted by an attack that stealthily drains their batteries, leaving cellular communications networks useless, according to computer security researchers at the University of California-- Davis (UC Davis). 'Battery power is the bottleneck for a cell phone,' said Hao Chen, assistant professor of computer science at UC Davis. 'It can't do anything with a dead battery.' Cell phones are designed to conserve battery life by spending most of their time in standby mode. Chen, and graduate students Denys Ma and Radmilo Racic, found that the MMS [Microsoft Media Server] protocol, which allows cell phones to send and receive pictures, video and audio files, can be used to send packets of junk data to a cell phone. Every time the phone receives one of these packets, it 'wakes up' from standby mode, but quickly discards the junk packet without ringing or alerting the user. Deprived of sleep by repeated pulses of junk data, the phone's batteries run down up to 20 times faster than in regular use. The attacker needs to know the number and Internet address of the victim's cell phone, but those are easy to obtain, Chen said. The computer used to launch the attack could be anywhere on the Internet. Chen and his students have tested the concept in the laboratory. They have also found other vulnerabilities in the MMS protocol -- one, for example, would allow users to circumvent billing for multimedia services and send files for free. As cell phone

cyber attack. Viewing SMiShing[216] as an example, this is a mobile device attack that seeks to dupe the recipient of an SMS (short message service – text) message into downloading malware onto their handset.[217] Once the handset is infected, it can be turned into a "zombie," allowing attackers to control the device.[218] If the mobile device communicates with any computers, they too can be infected and become nodes on a "zombie botnet."[219]

Analysts predict these and other threats of various types to cell phones and other mobile devices will eventually outnumber malware-laden e-mail messages.[220] In addition, these attacks can be used to expand their own scope to personal computers (PCs) and other networks when unsuspecting users forward these messages to their PCs.[221] Researchers have been able to demonstrate this style of attack scenario with no user involvement or action at all using only SMS messages.

These types of attacks on our cell phone infrastructure require very little in the way of resources, making them ideal candidates for malicious actors. The primary vehicle for the attack is the software that links the cell phones to their network, as the hardware is industry standard and already in most cell phones. These attacks illustrate the enormous impact that standards play vis-à-vis vulnerabilities that may affect communications security. If certain specific hardware and software standards were nationalized and closed, the ability for attackers to exploit specific national networks would be greatly reduced. By utilizing open standards, even in secure applications, it becomes an easier proposition for malicious actors, state affiliated or otherwise, to cripple the wireless communication networks of other countries.

The Debate Over "Open" vs. "Closed" Standards

The question of whether to adopt "open" or "closed" standards has sparked debate in the realm of cyber security. Proponents of closed standards believe their way is most secure because it is most secret; proponents of open standards believe their way is most secure because it allows their vulnerabilities to be identified, for users to be informed, and for systems to be tested quickly and broadly for malware infections.

---

providers offer more services, such as e-mail, web surfing and file sharing, they become vulnerable to the same attacks as computers, as well as to new types of attack that exploit their specific vulnerabilities. 'It's important to evaluate security now, while cell phones are being connected to the broadband Internet,' Chen said." http://www.sciencedaily.com/releases/2006/08/060829090243.htm.

[216] Washington State Office of the Attorney General, "Cell Phones Under Attack: How to block text spam and viruses," December 19, 2007: "Cell phones with Internet access are especially at risk. By clicking on a link in a smishing message, you can unknowingly allow a hacker to steal your personal information, activate your phone's camera or even listen in on your private cell phone conversations. In some cases, these programs can send fake messages to people in a phone's contact list. Last year, techies discovered a Trojan horse program that pretended to access Web pages but instead sent SMS messages to premium-rate phone numbers -- costing the cell phone user. Another message offered victims free antivirus software for their phone, supposedly from their mobile service provider. Users that downloaded the software from the link were infected with malware." http://www.sciencedaily.com/releases/2006/08/060829090243.htm.

[217] TechTarget, "SMiShing," SearchMobileComputing.com, Definitions. http://searchmobilecomputing.techtarget.com/sDefinition/0,,sid40_gci1241308,00.html.

[218] TechTarget, "SMiShing," SearchMobileComputing.com, Definitions. http://searchmobilecomputing.techtarget.com/sDefinition/0,,sid40_gci1241308,00.html.

[219] TechTarget, "SMiShing," SearchMobileComputing.com, Definitions. http://searchmobilecomputing.techtarget.com/sDefinition/0,,sid40_gci1241308,00.html.

[220] TechTarget, "SMiShing," SearchMobileComputing.com, Definitions. http://searchmobilecomputing.techtarget.com/sDefinition/0,,sid40_gci1241308,00.html.

[221] TechTarget, "SMiShing," SearchMobileComputing.com, Definitions. http://searchmobilecomputing.techtarget.com/sDefinition/0,,sid40_gci1241308,00.html.

Current cyber research is revealing that the majority of analyzed cyber intrusions utilize techniques and/or vulnerabilities that are not patchable in the contemporary sense (i.e., updating software to remain current). In other words, there may at times be a likelihood that security software or updates (whether open or closed) will not address the most commonly used vectors of targeted attacks and will offer little or no protection from them. Also apparent is that the majority of analyzed attacks are committed using "old" means based on tools or techniques that have been in the wild for months or years. The duration of cyber attacks also seems to be increasing, with cyber-intruders persistently and dynamically present and undetected on systems for months or years.

Therefore, a flexible, thoughtful, and informed hybrid approach to security that effectively uses simple tools (both open and closed as they demonstrate merit) may be the most meaningful approach to security.[222]

Mainstream wireless communications-based attacks could have significant economic impacts as well as negatively impacting national security by potentially limiting or eliminating the ability of defenders to communicate effectively. In the past, cell phones have generally been regarded as immune from viruses, worms, Trojan horses, or other malware that have threatened PC-based networks for years. However, that has changed with the targeting of high-end phones with fully functional operating systems and the ability to download and install a wide variety of applications. The biggest culprit leading to infection by viruses or Trojans is the downloading of files, applications, ringtones, games, and other related content.

Mobile devices are capable of carrying a virus back to a PC when the two devices synchronize. A mobile user could pick up a virus outside a network perimeter on the mobile device, bring it back inside a firewall, and synchronize it with a system on their network, spreading the virus on an otherwise secure local area network (LAN), then a wide area network (WAN), and beyond. As an example of another potential vulnerability, a Trojan horse application can be installed on a device through memory cards, infrared file transfer, or synchronization. An attacker can send a special text message to the infected phone, signaling the Trojan to commit a hostile act such as stealing the last five minutes of phone conversation stored in the device's memory.

In a demonstration presented at the Black Hat Security Conference in Las Vegas in July 2009, researchers revealed that an attacker could exploit a software hole to make calls, steal data, send text messages, and do more or less anything a person can do on their iPhone.[223] The attacker needed only to send SMS control messages to the device and could then send SMS messages to anyone in the victim's address book to spread the attack.[224] This attack required no effort of the part of the user and only looked for the victim's phone number.[225] The attacker sends SMS messages containing configuration information that is normally found only on network servers.[226] According to reports, Global System for Mobile Communications (GSM)

[222] Reperi LLC, information, technology, and telecommunications security research, supported variously by other sources.
[223] Elinor Mills, "Researchers take control of iPhone via SMS," ZDNet.com, July 30, 2009. http://news.zdnet.com/2100-9595_22-326501.html.
[224] Elinor Mills, "Researchers take control of iPhone via SMS," ZDNet.com, July 30, 2009. http://news.zdnet.com/2100-9595_22-326501.html.
[225] Elinor Mills, "Researchers take control of iPhone via SMS," ZDNet.com, July 30, 2009. http://news.zdnet.com/2100-9595_22-326501.html.
[226] Robert McMillan, "Some SMS Networks Vulnerable to Attack," July 28, 2009. http://tech.yahoo.com/news/pcworld/20090729/tc_pcworld/somesmsnetworksvulnerabletoattack.

networks are susceptible, but CDMA networks are not.[227] Other bugs found in cell phone software have allowed attackers to control the user interface on Windows Mobile devices via the SMS messages to disable keypads, rendering the cell phone unusable.[228]

Prior to this report, another similar type attack was reported by Trust Digital in April 2009.[229] In this type of attack, an SMS message is sent to a phone that opens its browser directing the phone to a malicious website; the website then downloads software to the phone and steals the information on the phone.[230] In a paper written by Penn State University researchers in 2005, various SMS vulnerabilities were identified, details of how the SMS attacks could be accomplished were described, and mitigation recommendations were presented.[231]

Reports have indicated that three China-based entities created the "Sexy Space" Trojan and tried to send it through the Symbian Foundation's digital-signing process.[232] All Symbian Series 60 third-edition phones by Nokia, LG, and Samsung were potential targets of the malware.[233] At the time of original reference, the Symbian platform was in use in just under 50 percent of all smart phones.[234]

Another potential national threat involving the iPhone and the exclusive AT&T wireless network has been dubbed "Jailbreaking."[235] The lighter side of Jailbreaking involves users who want to break free from carrier and manufacturer restrictions to use software they prefer,[236] but it may also have more serious implications. Jailbreaking alters a phone's baseband processor (BBP) that facilitates connections to cell towers,[237] meaning that attackers could potentially disable those towers.[238] Changing the BBP code can also allow the Exclusive Chip Identification (ECID) to be changed, making the device essentially anonymous on the network.[239] These vulnerabilities in cell phones can be easily exploited with a computer, access to a WiFi network,

---

[227] Robert McMillan, "Some SMS Networks Vulnerable to Attack," July 28, 2009. *http://tech.yahoo.com/news/pcworld/20090729/tc_pcworld/somesmsnetworksvulnerabletoattack*; and also Jim Dalrymple , "Apple Fixes iPhone SMS Flaw," July 31 2009. *http://news.cnet.com/8301-1009_3-10301001-83.html.*
[228] Elinor Mills, "Researchers take control of iPhone via SMS," ZDNet.com, July 30, 2009. *http://news.zdnet.com/2100-9595_22-326501.html.*
[229] Elinor Mills, "SMS Messages Could Be Used to Hijack a Phone," April 19, 2009. *http://news.cnet.com/8301-1009_3-10222921-83.html.*
[230] Elinor Mills, "SMS Messages Could Be Used to Hijack a Phone," April 19, 2009. *http://news.cnet.com/8301-1009_3-10222921-83.html.*
[231] William Enck et al.,"Exploiting Open Functionality in SMS-Capable Cellular Networks," (Pennsylvania State University, September 2, 2005). *http://www.smsanalysis.org/smsanalysis.pdf.*
[232] Vivian Yeo, "Chinese Firms Behind 'Sexy Space' Trojan," July 22, 2009. *http://news.cnet.com/8301-1009_3-10292917-83.html.*
[233] Vivian Yeo, "Chinese Firms Behind 'Sexy Space' Trojan," July 22, 2009. *http://news.cnet.com/8301-1009_3-10292917-83.html* .
[234] Vivian Yeo, "Chinese Firms Behind 'Sexy Space' Trojan," July 22, 2009. *http://news.cnet.com/8301-1009_3-10292917-83.html* .
[235] Dong Ngo, "Jailbreaking iPhone could pose threat to national security, Apple claims," July 29, 2009. *http://reviews.cnet.com/8301-19512_7-10298646-233.html*; David Kravets, "iPhone Jailbreaking Could Crash Cellphone Towers, Apple Claims," Wired.com, July 28, 2009. *http://www.wired.com/threatlevel/2009/07/jailbreak/.*
[236] David Kravets, "iPhone Jailbreaking Could Crash Cellphone Towers, Apple Claims," Wired.com, July 28, 2009. *http://www.wired.com/threatlevel/2009/07/jailbreak/*
[237] David Kravets, "iPhone Jailbreaking Could Crash Cellphone Towers, Apple Claims," Wired.com, July 28, 2009. *http://www.wired.com/threatlevel/2009/07/jailbreak/* .
[238] David Kravets, "iPhone Jailbreaking Could Crash Cellphone Towers, Apple Claims," Wired.com, July 28, 2009. *http://www.wired.com/threatlevel/2009/07/jailbreak/*..
[239] David Kravets, "iPhone Jailbreaking Could Crash Cellphone Towers, Apple Claims," Wired.com, July 28, 2009. *http://www.wired.com/threatlevel/2009/07/jailbreak/.*

a couple of cell phones, and a business card.[240] These types of attacks are on the rise and, given the speed with which information moves via the Internet, it becomes a challenge for the industry to close the holes before the next ones are discovered.[241]

From a communications security perspective, government procurement of cell phones might appropriately consider both the hardware and software aspects of devices. Vulnerabilities associated with hardware may relate to overreliance on particular networks, and/or overreliance of supply chains on particular hardware supply models. One potential mitigation strategy is for the Department of Defense and other government organizations to consider the use of cell phones that are flexible in both data transmission standards and physical hardware -- which is to say, easily replaceable and able to function across multiple network types and spectrum bands/frequencies. Reliance on particular hardware designs could have negative impacts if the supplier(s) fail, withhold production, or otherwise undermine systems or services, or if consequent supply chains suffer disruptions or failure.[242]

Reliance on a particular transmission standard would limit the field of use to the range of compatible networks. By using a broad spectrum purchasing approach, security can be enhanced by having utilization capabilities across a wide variety of hardware and data transmission protocols. This would enable the supply chain to adapt to many adverse situations. Mobile devices are relatively inexpensive and easily moved from region to region. However, alternative approaches, consisting of closed networks and proprietary hardware, tend to be costly and ineffective from an economic and mobility standpoint. Manufacturers are often reluctant to dedicate scarce resources to pursue such technology models if they will lack broad market appeal.

From a software perspective, cell phone technology is changing and evolving every day. Attacks from a wide variety of vectors will only increase. The first step to mitigate these attacks should be increased user education and awareness. Comprehensive training on what to look for and how attackers are utilizing new technologies would improve the process of attack identification and prevention. Identifying when a device or network has been compromised is the fastest way of taking evasive action to close the device, move to another device, or utilize a different network. Having immediate access to source code for device operating systems and network software is another tactic to pursue to avoid delay in heading off cellular attacks. In addition to having the source code access, trained personnel are required to make lightning-fast adjustments to source code bases both to defend against and pursue attackers.

Smart phones blend the voice and data features of both phones and personal digital assistants (PDAs) into a single portable device. Many of today's wireless handsets include calendars, alarms, and downloadable applications and typically support e-mail and desktop synchronization so that mobile users have access to their master contact, calendar, and to-do lists. Wireless handsets have evolved into a technology that offers near-constant access for multimedia applications such as global positioning system (GPS), video gaming, stereo FM radio, digital photography, CD (compact disc)-quality music, texting, access to e-mail, Internet browsing, and many other functions. While such functions can contribute greatly to both professional productivity and personal entertainment, the ready connectivity of handset devices opens many more potential doors to malicious network actors.

---

[240] Joan Goodchild, "3 Simple Steps to Hack a Cell Phone," CSO Online, April 29, 2009. http://www.csoonline.com/article/491200/_Simple_Steps_to_Hack_a_Smartphone_Includes_Video.
[241] Joan Goodchild, "CISCO: SMS Smartphone Attacks on the Rise," CSO Online, July 14, 2009. http://www.csoonline.com/article/497120/Cisco_SMS_Smartphone_Attacks_on_the_Rise.
[242] Reperi LLC, "Trends In Mobile Wireless Communications," 2006.

WIRELESS HEADSETS, EARPIECES, AND BLUETOOTH

Almost all of China's phone manufacturers make Bluetooth products. ZTE makes Bluetooth accessories to go with its mobile phone products, some of which may have limited market penetration in the United States but which could be part of any larger agreement with major U.S. telecommunications carriers. Bluetooth is an open wireless technology that allows wireless devices to exchange data over short distances. In essence, when Bluetooth devices connect to one another, they create a small wireless personal area network (PAN). Multiple devices can be connected to the same PAN. Bluetooth is a ubiquitous standard today, so most Chinese manufacturers do produce Bluetooth devices. Bluetooth uses frequency-hopping spread-spectrum radio technology, which breaks up data and spreads data out on up to 79 different frequencies, transmitting about a megabit of data per second. Connections can be made and information exchanged between any devices that are Bluetooth capable.

Bluetooth: Potential Vulnerabilities

When Bluetooth is enabled, it generally is configured to broadcast its device's availability for a connection to any and all other devices in range, which makes the device very easy for an attacker to locate and exploit. An attacker need only be equipped with the required software and a portable computer with a Bluetooth adapter. The attacker need only go into an area where they expect to find targetable devices nearby and then perform their attack automatically when vulnerable devices are located. With the attacker's system scanning for targets automatically, the attacker can remain inconspicuous, and the nature of the attacks generally will not alert the victim to the fact that they are under attack.

Once a device is compromised, the attacker can gain access to all data and system functionality. A large number of programs are available that are specifically designed to attack Bluetooth cell phones. "Bluesnarfing" is the common term for an attack that downloads all of the victim's data, while "Bluebugging" is an attack that allows the attacker to turn a compromised wireless phone into a bugging device or to eavesdrop on all calls made on the device.

Compromised phones can be used for a myriad of purposes, from collecting private or sensitive information, diverting long distance charges, and eavesdropping, to rigging them with kill commands or other damaging exploits.

Switching Equipment and Other Networking Services – The Nortel Story

Nortel Company Logo

From its founding in 1895 as Northern Electric and Manufacturing, and its early days of manufacturing equipment for Canada's fledgling telephone system,[243] Nortel grew to become a major manufacturer of telecom equipment ranging from carrier-class systems to user equipment (much of it deployed throughout the U.S. government). Beginning in the early 2000s, Nortel started to experience financial difficulties and began exploring deals with other corporations:

---

[243] Nortel.com website, "Nortel History." *http://www.nortel.com/corporate/corptime/index.html.*

-- In 2004, Nortel and China Putian Corporation[244] agreed to a memorandum of understanding for cooperation on research and development, and manufacture of 3G equipment and products. The two companies cooperated on projects such as 3G field trials sponsored by China's Ministry of Information Industry.

-- In 2005, Nortel and China Putian established a joint venture for research and development, manufacturing, and sale of 3G mobile telecom equipment and products to customers in China. Signing of the Joint Venture Framework Agreement occurred in Beijing and was witnessed by China's Premier Wen Jiabao and Canada's Prime Minister Paul Martin.[245]

-- In February 2006, Nortel and Huawei announced plans to form a joint venture in order to develop IP broadband internet solutions.[246] This venture evidently did not progress beyond the early stages.

-- In 2008 – a year in which the company's stock lost 96 percent of its value and the company was mulling bankruptcy[247] – a possible deal emerged that would have resulted in an infusion of much-needed cash into the company. Huawei bid $400 million for Nortel's Metro Ethernet Networking business, a bid that some industry observers considered far above its value.[248] However, concerns over Huawei's background appear to have derailed the deal, with some U.S. broadband providers reportedly indicating that they would stop buying Nortel equipment if Huawei acquired a large stake in the firm.[249]

-- On January 14, 2009, Nortel sought bankruptcy protection.[250] Since this time, a general sell-off of Nortel's business units and assets has occurred.[251] Telefonaktiebolaget LM Ericsson ("Ericsson"), Kapsch CarrierCom AG ("Kapsch"), Ciena, GENBAND, Inc., Avaya Inc., and Hitachi Ltd. have each purchased portions of Nortel or its assets and subsidiaries, constituting the bulk of the company.[252]

---

[244] Hoovers.com reference. *http://www.hoovers.com/company/CHINA_PUTIAN_CORPORATION/rfjhhif-1.html*.

[245] Press release on the Nortel.com website. *http://www.nortel.com/corporate/news/newsreleases/2005a/01_20_05_china_putian.html*.

[246] Nortel.com, "Nortel, Huawei to Establish Joint Venture to Address Broadband Access Market" and "Plan to Jointly Develop Ultra Broadband Products for Delivery of Converged Services," February 1, 2006. *http://www2.nortel.com/go/news_detail.jsp?cat_id=-8055&oid=100194923*.

[247] Andy Greenberg, "Nortel's China Syndrome," *Forbes.com*, January 12, 2009. *http://www.forbes.com/2009/01/11/nortel-huawei-buyout-tech-enter-cx_ag_0112nortel.html*.

[248] Andy Greenberg, "Nortel's China Syndrome," *Forbes.com*, January 12, 2009. *http://www.forbes.com/2009/01/11/nortel-huawei-buyout-tech-enter-cx_ag_0112nortel.html*.

[249] Andy Greenberg, "Nortel's China Syndrome," *Forbes.com*, January 12, 2009. *http://www.forbes.com/2009/01/11/nortel-huawei-buyout-tech-enter-cx_ag_0112nortel.html*.

[250] Lionel Laurent, "Nortel Throws in the Towel," *Forbes.com*, January 14, 2009. *http://www.forbes.com/2009/01/14/nortel-alcatel-technology-markets-equity-cx_ll_0114markets11.html?partner=whiteglove_google*.

[251] Nortel.com, "Nortel Obtains Court Orders for Creditor Protection," January 14, 2009. *http://www2.nortel.com/go/news_detail.jsp?cat_id=-8055&oid=100251347&locale=en-US*; and Nortel.com, "Nortel Business and Financial Restructuring," *http://www.nortel.com/corporate/restructuring.html*; and Nortel's U.S. claims agent, Epiq Bankruptcy Solutions, LLC. *http://chapter11.epiqsystems.com/NNI/Project/default.aspx?DMWin=dcd9aa35-e94e-418b-84a3-d769f095df78*.

[252] Based on data available from the Nortel.com website, restructuring section. *http://www.nortel.com/corporate/restructuring.html*.

The Nortel Story as a Possible Sign of Things to Come

In the example of the abortive Huawei/Nortel deal, we see what is likely to become a repeating pattern in both the telecom and other industries:

1. A western telecom company with a very strong and deep business posture in the U.S. marketplace in general (and the U.S. government in specific) begins to experience distress related to prevailing economic conditions;

2. The company accepts research and development ties with Chinese companies in an effort to gain large-scale entry into China's lucrative new market but finds that the benefits of entering the Chinese market fail to provide the new lease on life that is hoped for;

3. A Chinese company flush with investment capital (Huawei) steps in to purchase portions of the distressed company's (Nortel) business in which it is interested (also giving the distressed company an infusion of much-needed cash);

4. However, push-back from the distressed company's customers (due to security concerns) can be sufficient to discourage the deal. Numerous restructuring efforts may then fail to achieve sufficient positive traction, and the distressed company may subsequently wind up in bankruptcy.

At present, Nortel is being sold in parts to the highest bidders.

TABLE 1: WHERE CHINA'S PRODUCTS ARE FOUND IN THE U.S. COMMUNICATIONS MARKET

WHAT IT IS: PRODUCT	WHO MAKES IT: MANUFACTURER	WHAT IT IS USED FOR, AND WHAT IT CAN DO	PRESENT OR FUTURE USE	SOURCE
ZTE EV-DO Modem/USB	ZTE, relabeled by Verizon and other companies	Connecting wirelessly to 3G, GSM, EDGE, and HSDPA (High-Speed Downlink Packet Access)	Compatible with wireless networks like Verizon, AT&T	engadgetmobile.com
ZTE Smartphones/3G, 4G with Qwerty keyboards, LTE devices	ZTE USA; planned partnership with Verizon Wireless	Competes with other wireless handset providers	Competes with Apple, Blackberry (RIM), Motorola, and other handset providers, Nokia, Ericsson, and Samsung	fiercewireless.com
Application Software for Wireless Devices – TechSoft Mobile Solutions Suite	QualComm/China TechFaith joint venture wireless company – each put in up to~$35 million, according to reports. The new company is China-based TechSoft. TechFaith was Qualcomm's first independent design house partner	Operating software for CDMA mobile handsets *http://www.techfaithwireless.com/english/products/products_ApplicationSoftware.htm*	3G CDMA mobile handset software applications	Electronics News, 03/27/2008
Base Station and equipment for HSDPA (high-speed downlink packet access)	Huawei – Provider to T-Mobile – *in Europe – working on a deal for U.S.*	Base station for wireless networks allowing maximized use of towers/cabinets in rolling out HSDPA, reducing build-out costs for T-Mobile. HSDPA is a packet-based mobile telephony protocol used in 3G UMTS (universal mobile telecommunications system) radio networks to increase data capacity and speed up transfer rates.	Deployment in cellular, GSM, and wireless networks, provides access to data packets	Network World
Patent for WiMAX wireless patents	Nokia Siemens Network/Nokia parent company and Huawei – patent deal	Deal covers standards relating to GSM, WCDMA, CDMA, optical networking, datacom, and WiMAX	Standards control	telecoms.com
Huawei E583 X Modem	3G to WiFi Huawei	It is what T-Mobile and other network providers would like to offer	Mobile network connectivity for individual users	CNET SlashGear
3G Network Equipment/LTE Ready	Huawei	4G and 3G networks – wireless. Cox wireless network	Deployment in U.S. cities	*Wall Street Journal* Network World

TABLE 2: WHERE CHINA'S INVESTMENTS ARE FOUND IN THE U.S. COMMUNICATIONS MARKET

The table below highlights significant Chinese investments in the U.S. telecommunications sector. This table also lists some attempted deals that failed to obtain CFIUS approval. Even though some of the deals noted below did not go through, it is important to note that these investment attempts had the potential for impacting key network traffic important to U.S. national security interests.

INVESTOR	INVESTMENT	WHAT IT IS/PART OF SUPPLY CHAIN	WHAT IT DOES/CAN DO	INVESTMENT AMOUNT	DATE	SOURCE
Hutchison Whampoa	Joint venture with Global Crossing 50/50.[253] Total: both partners $1.2 billion	Fiber routes. Fixed line telecommuni-cations. Internet, fiber optic, international cable. Web hosting.	Provide international telecom transport – network monitoring.	Aggregate joint venture value of $1.2 billion.	2000	Highbeam.com Hutchison Whampoa Press Release
Hutchison Whampoa – Singapore Telecom STT	Assets of Global Crossing (Asian Crossing).[254]	Undersea cable traffic to U.S.	Carry traffic between U.S., Asia, Europe, and some continental U.S. routes	$250 Million *Deal went forward with Singapore Telecom Only	2002	SEC 10K
Huawei Bain Capital Partners and Huawei jointly	Acquisition attempt. 51/49 percent majority in Huawei 3-Com (H3C). 3-Com later bought out the joint venture.[255]	Wireless routers, voice, data, networking products. Proposed buyout for $2.2 billion of 3Com in 2007 – U.S. government objected; acquisition failed. 3Com revenues have spiraled downward since.	Wireless data traffic transport. Routers for DOD and federal government.	Unknown.	2003 - 2007.	Press Releases
Cox Com	Huawei	LTE and wireless base stations.	Broadband communications.	Undisclosed	2009	*Wall Street Journal*
Leap Wireless "Cricket"	Huawei	CDMA / EV-DO networking products. Huawei CDMA2000 network with 1xEV-DO Rev A capable BTS (base transceiver	Wireless broadband modems, routers. Broadband data transmission.	Undisclosed	2009	EETimes Asia.Com

[253] Hutchison Whampoa Limited Press Release, "Hutchison Whampoa and Global Crossing complete telecom joint venture in Hong Kong," January 12, 2000.

[254] Global Crossing SEC (Securities and Exchange Commission) 10K Filing, 2002.

[255] 3-Com later bought out its portion of the H3C joint venture.

		station). The solutions will include Huawei's SoftX3000-Softswitch, Air Bridge BSC6600, UMG8900-Universal Media Gateway, and high-capacity BTS 3606.				
Clearwire (investors, Intel, Sprint Nextel, Google)	Huawei	WiMAX. 4G networks. WiMAX base stations. LTE.	High-speed broadband wireless.	Undisclosed	2009	*Wall Street Journal*
Verizon	ZTE	USB modems.	Data Comm.	Unknown	2007	Newswire

Figure 6: Sample Integrated Operational Network Model (Healthy)

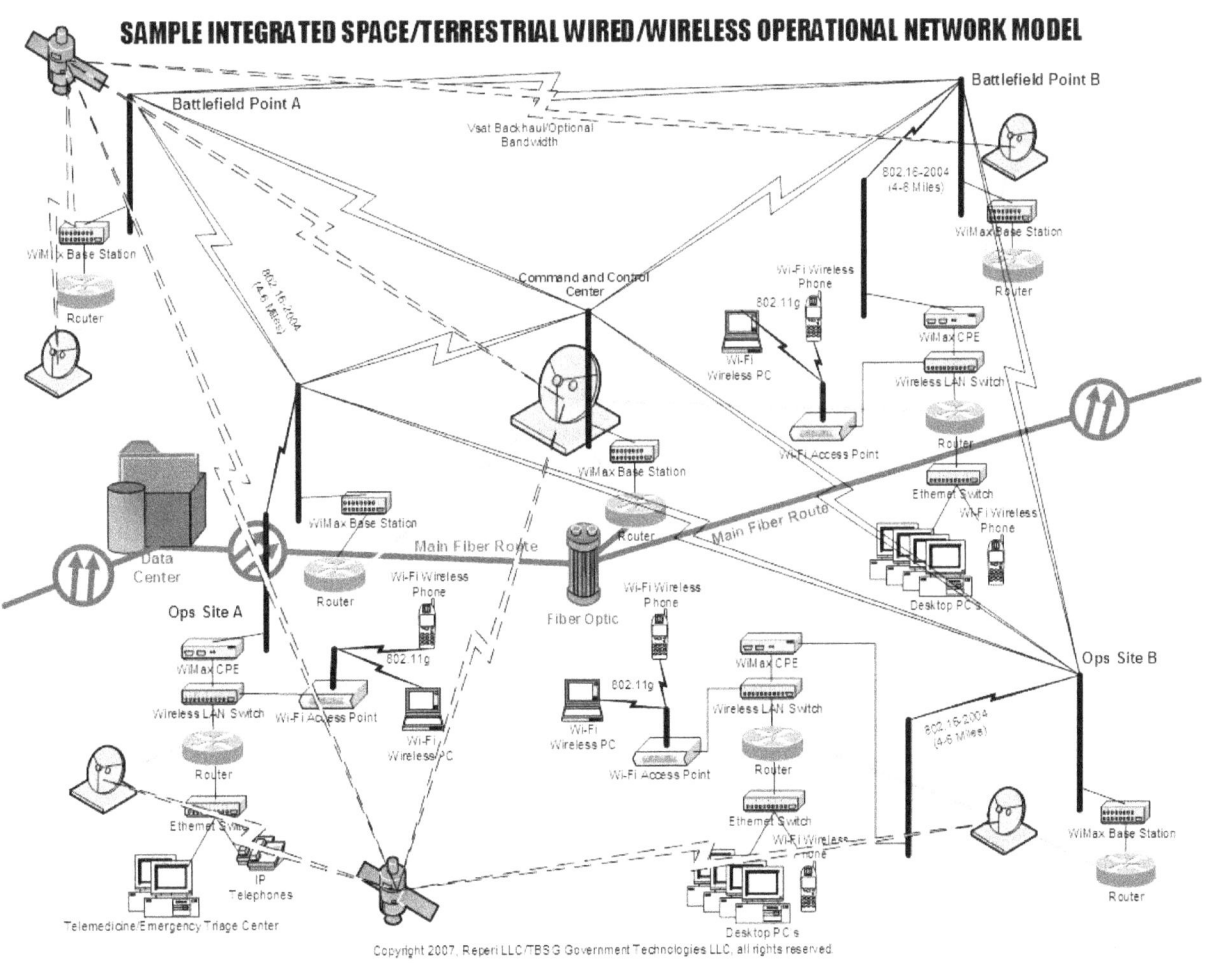

Figure 7: Sample Integrated Operational Network Model (Corrupted)

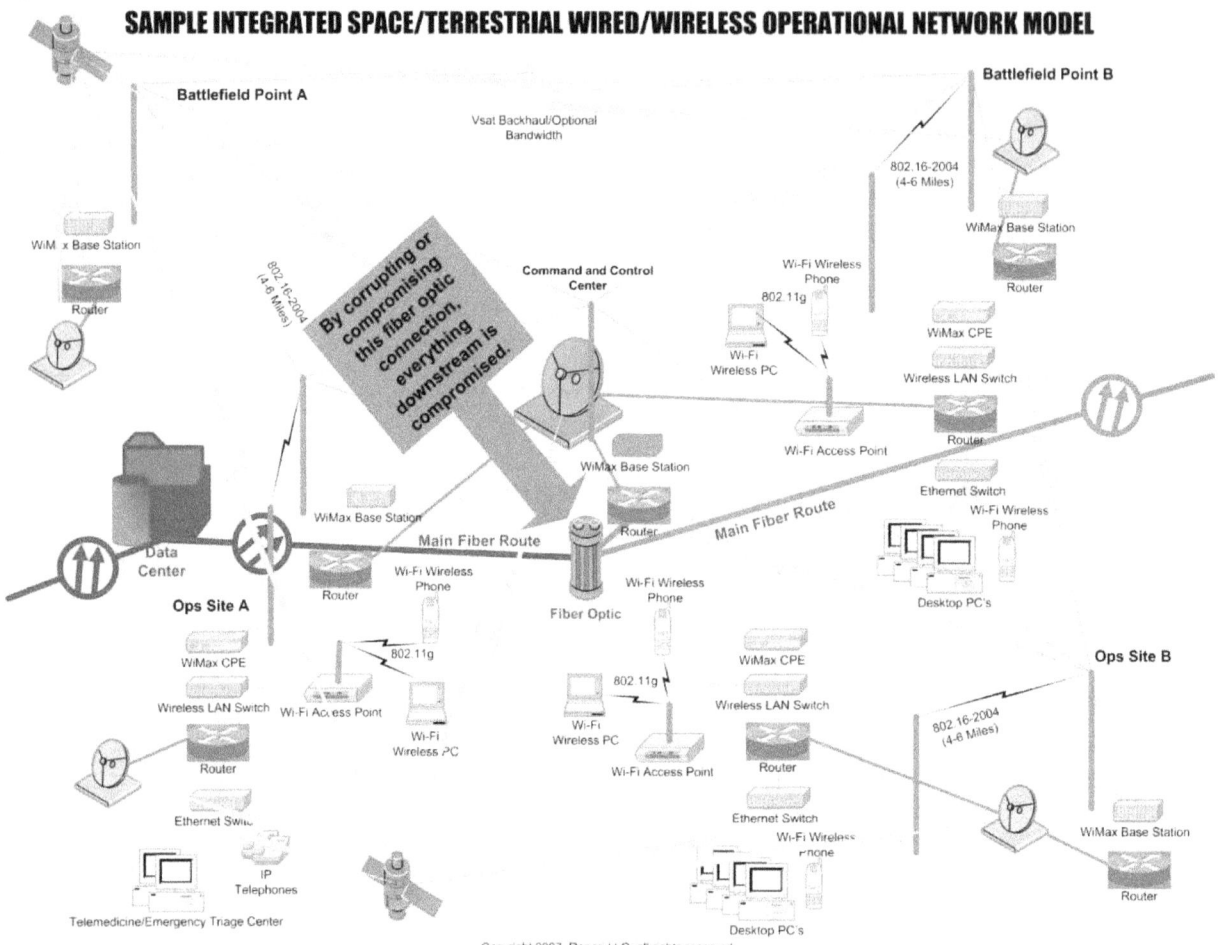

60

Figure 8: Sample Integrated Operational Network Model (Disabled)[256]

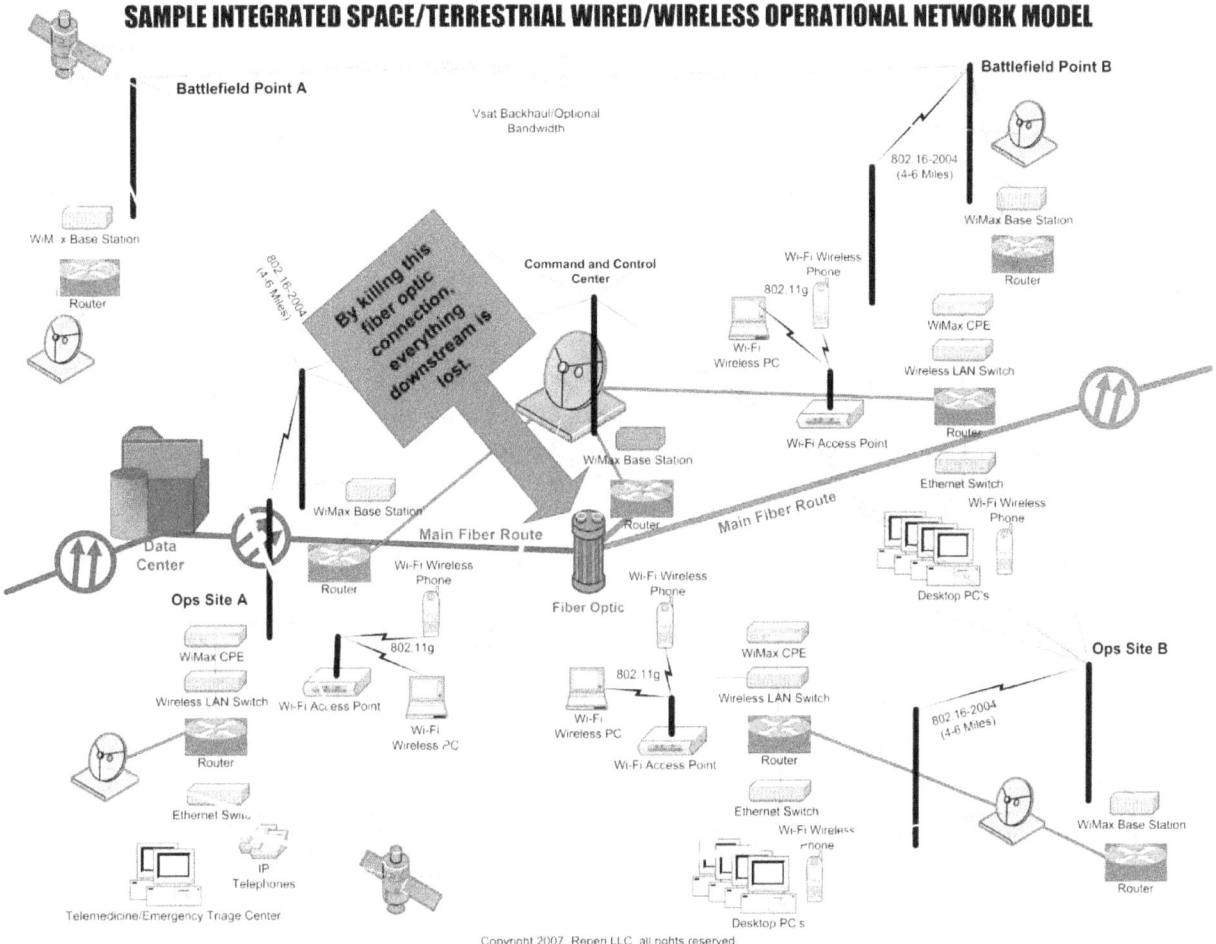

SAMPLE INTEGRATED SPACE/TERRESTRIAL WIRED/WIRELESS OPERATIONAL NETWORK MODEL

---

[256] A useful reference for additional perspective is the war impact maps of the Serbian networks during their 1999 conflict, available at *http://www.cheswick.com/ches/map/yu/index.html.*

SECTION 3
SUPPLY CHAIN INTEGRITY, AND THE IMPACT ON GOVERNMENT / DEFENSE CONTRACTING

American interests are heavily dependent on cyber space and, in the case of businesses and private individuals, many vital functions are now tied together across private or public networks such as the Internet. In the case of national security and defense enterprises, cyberspace is also now a key enabler. Continuously available secure enterprise networks are indispensable and now reside at the core of national security mission needs.

> *The loss of unfettered access to cyberspace would not merely be "game changing" in America, it would be profoundly catastrophic. Cyberspace is a crown jewel at our national core that should be protected with care. American awareness of the critical value of cyberspace is growing, but not at a pace that is commensurate with the rate at which cyber risks are increasing.*
>
> The most pressing critical strategic cyber security issues are the following:
>
> - Recognition by policymakers of the need to adapt quickly to address and fund critical vulnerabilities.
> - Substantial security risks posed by critical supply chain vulnerabilities due to dependence on foreign innovation and manufacturing.
> - Potentials for permanent loss of critical supply chain elements.

The U.S. Department of Defense has recognized cyber security as a principal issue and is seeking to address it in both policy and practice. Admirable efforts to address culture, management, and technical challenges are being undertaken in the U.S. defense community in response to the growing awareness of the criticality of cyberspace.[257] However, given the context of resources and policy, U.S. military efforts are necessarily focused first on the tremendous challenge of protecting and enabling military cyberspace, while the vast majority of American critical cyberspace existing in the private/commercial realm remains largely unaddressed by government cyber security efforts.

The question of supply chain security is a key element in cyber security. Dependency upon foreign manufacturers for critical products across the telecommunications, communications, and information systems supply chains impacts almost every aspect of voice and data transport. To date, public discussion of the vulnerabilities of electronics components to malicious tampering has been largely theoretical, but historical precedent does exist:

> *At the height of the cold war, in June 1982, an American early-warning satellite detected a large blast in Siberia... [It was] an explosion on a Soviet gas pipeline. The cause was a malfunction in the computer-control system that Soviet spies had stolen from a firm in Canada. They did not know that the CIA [Central Intelligence Agency] had tampered with*

---

[257] House Armed Services Committee, Subcommittee on Terrorism, Unconventional Threats, and Capabilities, Statement by Michael E. Krieger, deputy chief information officer/G-6, United States Army, 111th Cong., 2nd sess., May 5, 2009.

the software so that it would 'go haywire, after a decent interval, to reset pump speeds and valve settings to produce pressures far beyond those acceptable to pipeline joints and welds,' according to the memoirs of Thomas Reed, a former air force secretary. The result, he said, 'was the most monumental non-nuclear explosion and fire ever seen from space.'…

… given that computer chips and software are produced globally, could a foreign power infect high-tech military equipment with computer bugs? 'It scares me to death,' says one senior military source. 'The destructive potential is so great.'[258]

If agents of the U.S. government could maliciously tamper with electronics components bound for purchase by an adversary, then adversaries of the United States could certainly consider doing the same. This may already have happened in at least one instance: Jim Lewis, an expert on cyber security issues at the Center for Strategic and International Studies, has described a case of sabotaged hardware that may have been used to facilitate a breach of secure systems at the U.S. Central Command in 2008. As stated in an interview with CBS News:

Last November, someone was able to get past the firewalls and encryption devices of one of the most sensitive U.S. military computer systems and stay inside for several days. 'This was the CENTCOM network,' Lewis explained. '[S]ome foreign power was able to get into their networks. They could see what the traffic was. They could read documents. They could interfere with things. It was like they were part of the American military command.'

Lewis believes it was done by foreign spies who left corrupted thumbnail drives or memory sticks lying around in places where U.S. military personnel were likely to pick them up. As soon as someone inserted one into a CENTCOM computer, a malicious code opened a backdoor for the foreign power to get into the system.[259]

Supply Chain Integrity and Cyber Security

Loss of control of telecommunications supply chains could constitute one of the single greatest threats to U.S. cyber and communications security. *There are many potentially troubling issues surrounding potential corruption and/or tampering with electronics manufacturing supply chains. These include the following:*

- Potential increased risk of loss of sensitive data and intellectual property through compromised networks;
- Impacts of a potential adversary's reach into critical infrastructure and weapons systems for sabotage;
- Loss of manufacturing, infrastructure, scientific, and engineering expertise.

Exposure and national security risks should be evaluated from a variety of factors:

- The loss of U.S. dominance or competitiveness in the overall context of the national security supply chains or in key individual segments.
- The loss of supply chain components.

---

[258] *Economist*, "War in the Fifth Domain," July 1, 2010.
[259] CBS News, *60 Minutes*, "Cyber War: Sabotaging the System,", November 8, 2009. *http://www.cbsnews.com/stories/2009/11/06/60minutes/main5555565.shtml.*

> - The ability of a foreign adversary to impact an element of the supply chain or resultant architectures through controllers and devices.
> - The means by which networks and devices move classified and nonclassified information.

Cyber security concern centering on China is a core issue that has created problems for Chinese telecom product suppliers on the global stage. As cited previously, India is selectively barring telecom deals with some foreign providers on this basis. In December 2009, India's Telecommunications Department asked Indian mobile phone operators to suspend deals with foreign equipment companies and told several mobile phone operators that proposed deals with Chinese companies could not proceed due to security concerns.[260] Central to India's concerns is the possibility of foreign malware, hacking, and spying. Restrictions have evidently been lifted on most foreign manufacturers, with those remaining under restriction being "principally Chinese."[261] Similar concerns came to light in the United Kingdom.[262] *(For further discussion of concerns by some governments regarding the alleged activities of Huawei, see p.16.)*

U.S. concerns in these respects are no less significant; however, American considerations are perhaps even more complex. As previously noted, there are significant, pervasive, and increasing interdependencies between the Chinese and American economies, particularly in the telecommunications sector. Potential U.S. cyber vulnerabilities are profound relative to our cyber defense capabilities. Research by cyber security professionals has illustrated U.S. cyber vulnerabilities and helped define the context of risks in terms of severity, magnitude, time indexes, and potential solutions.[263] Although collaboration with the private sector may be addressed in the Comprehensive National Cybersecurity Initiative,[264] the means of doing so may remain undefined and in need of exploration for some time. A major obstacle to meaningful public-private cooperative efforts is the absence of a common basis of knowledge and dialog to support operational working collaboration between the two sectors.

China's cyber warfare and cyber espionage capabilities are reported as being very substantial *(see text box on the following page),* with the potential for severe threats to both the integrity of government networks and to commercial intellectual property. Furthermore, with many U.S. business organizations doing business in China, it is no longer sufficient only to consider the circumstances of cyber security within the United States. Careful consideration of the ramifications (including impacts within the United States) of cyber vulnerabilities created by direct exposure to the Chinese marketplace is needed. Perhaps one of the best recent examples to cite is the controversy surrounding alleged penetrations of Google networks by

---

[260] *China Tech News,* "Indian Government Bans Import of Chinese Telecom Equipment,",April 30, 2010.

[261] Heather Timmons, "India Tells Mobile Firms to Delay Deals for Chinese Telecom Equipment," *New York Times,* April 30, 2010. *http://www.nytimes.com/2010/05/01/business/global/01delhi.html.*

[262] Michael Smith, "Spy chiefs fear Chinese cyber attack," *Sunday Times* (London), March 29, 2009. *http://www.timesonline.co.uk/tol/news/uk/article5993156.ece.*

[263] House Committee on Homeland Security, Subcommittee on Emerging Threats, Cybersecurity, and Science and Technology, "Addressing the Nation's Cyber Security Challenges: Reducing Vulnerabilities Requires Strategic Investment and Immediate Action," testimony of O. Sami Saydjari, president, Professionals for Cyber Defense, and chief executive officer, Cyber Defense Agency, LLC, 110th Cong., 1st sess., April 25, 2007. *http://homeland.house.gov/SiteDocuments/20070425145307-82503.pdf.*

[264] The White House: "The activities under way to implement the recommendations of the Cyberspace Policy Review build on the Comprehensive National Cybersecurity Initiative (CNCI) launched by President George W. Bush in National Security Presidential Directive 54/Homeland Security Presidential Directive 23 (NSPD-54/ HSPD-23) in January 2008. President Obama determined that the CNCI and its associated activities should evolve to become key elements of a broader, updated national U.S. cybersecurity strategy." *White House.gov,* May 2009.

Chinese hackers. U.S. telecommunications or technology companies with operations abroad may discover they are more vulnerable than expected.[265]

Chinese Cyber Espionage Directed vs. the United States

In a public report released in 2009, analysts with the Northrop Grumman Corporation produced a research report for the U.S.-China Economic and Security Review Commission that stated:

"China is likely using its maturing computer network exploitation capability to support intelligence collection against the US Government and industry by conducting a long-term, sophisticated, computer network exploitation campaign. The problem is characterized by disciplined, standardized operations, sophisticated techniques, access to high-end software development resources, a deep knowledge of the targeted networks, and an ability to sustain activities inside targeted networks, sometimes over a period of months."[266]

In early 2010, the computer security firm Mandiant released a report titled *The Advanced Persistent Threat*, which stated that:

"MANDIANT defines the APT [Advanced Persistent Threat] as a group of sophisticated, determined and coordinated attackers that have been systematically compromising U.S. government and commercial computer networks for years. The vast majority of APT activity observed by MANDIANT has been linked to China."[267]

CONTROL OF MANUFACTURING PROCESSES

Recent years have seen significant outsourcing of America's traditional manufacturing capacity. The impetus for such outsourcing is generally related to economics or more suitable operating environments (favorable tax treatments, government subsidies, less onerous labor laws, etc.), and these outsourcing opportunities can be very attractive to U.S. companies. Regardless, they can result in potential compromises to national security in a variety of ways, to include malicious intent or unintentional design or fabrication errors.

One of the dilemmas currently facing the American defense establishment is how to maintain both strategic and tactical superiority in an environment where the manufacture and provisioning of critical technology infrastructure is being outsourced rapidly to entities that may not have U.S. national interests foremost in their minds. In some cases, the loyalties of these entities may lie first with other nations, some of whom may have geopolitical goals that run contrary to those of the United States.

---

[265] Google, Inc., Google Beijing, Google Shanghai, Google Guangzhou, and Google Hong Kong; see also Dambala, Inc., "The Command Structure of the Aurora Botnet, History, Patterns and Findings," March 3, 2010.

[266] Northrop Grumman Corp., "Capability of the People's Republic of China to Conduct Cyber Warfare and Computer Network Exploitation" (paper produced for the U.S.-China Economic and Security Review Commission, October 2009). http://www.uscc.gov/researchpapers/2009/NorthropGrumman_PRC_Cyber_Paper_FINAL_Approved%20Report_16 Oct2009.pdf.

[267] Mandiant, "M Trends: The Advanced Persistent Threat," January 2010.

The United States has evolved a growing dependency on foreign suppliers for a number of critical electronics components. As noted earlier, Chinese manufacturers have achieved significant integration into the communications supply chain through varying forms of investment. As a result, they have obtained technological expertise, lower cost capabilities that allow "supply chain dominance," the ability not only to develop standards but also to dominate standards in many niches, and the ability to develop momentum in advancing development of next-generation technologies.[268]

Much of the U.S. economy and national well-being is irrevocably tied to the extensive system of voice, data, and video networks that tie together almost every fabric of our lives. This includes access to government information and services, contact with business associates, financial transactions, education, health care, management of utilities and other critical infrastructure, and social networking, among other baseline enabling functions. As technologies progress, the network continues to extend its reach to other devices, from the remotely monitored supervisory control and data acquisition (SCADA) systems that control public utilities, to personal electronics that allow remote activation of cell phones or other devices that can be accessed through or controlled by cell phones.[269] Disruptions, whether intentional or unintentional, can and do have profound consequences.

Lenovo Company Logo
Lenovo's Entry into the U.S. Computer Market, and Controversies Surrounding its Government Sales

Lenovo has emerged as one of the world's largest manufacturers of personal computers. Lenovo is headquartered in Purchase, New York, and manufactures in several locations in China as well as in Raleigh, North Carolina. The company began in 1984 as Legend Group, led by computer scientist Liu Chuanzhi. Legend originally received start-up capital from the Chinese Academy of Sciences, a government agency.[270] To date, Legend Holdings is the largest shareholder of Lenovo, and the Chinese Academy of Sciences owns 65 percent of Legend Holdings. In effect, the Chinese government is the largest shareholder in the company, though the extent of the government's role within the company is unclear.

In the 1990s, Lenovo served as the Chinese distributor for Hewlett-Packard Co. but has since expanded beyond manufacturing to information technology (IT) consulting, systems integration, software and e-commerce, mobile phones and personal digital assistants (PDA's). In 1994, the company listed on the Hong Kong Stock Exchange (HKSE: 0992) and is currently trading with a market capitalization of US$41.52 billion.[271] The company grew steadily over the last decade

[268] Reperi - General conclusion from the Defense Science Board Task Force on High-Performance Microchips Supply, February 2005, pp. 29-32.
[269] Reperi – It is reasonable to conclude that disruptions of this nature would have a profound and far-reaching detrimental effect.
[270] Lenovo Group Ltd., NOVEL NY Business & Company Resource Center, July 1, 2010. http://ezproxy.library.nyu.edu:2081/servlet/BCRC?vrsn=unknown&locID=nysl_me_nyuniv&srchtp=glbc&cc=1&c=1&mode=c&ste=74&tbst=tsCM&tab=4&ccmp=Lenovo+Group+Ltd.&mst=lenovo&n=25&docNum=I2501310652&bConts=13119.
[271] Yahoo! Finance, Lenovo Group Ltd. HKD0.025 (0992.HK), July 1, 2010. http://finance.yahoo.com/q?s=0992.HK.

through acquisition of IT consulting and systems integration systems. Legend was renamed The Lenovo Group in 2003.

Most famously, Lenovo acquired IBM's Personal Computing Division in 2005 for US$1.75 billion.[272] With the deal, Lenovo also acquired the right to IBM's Think Pad brand name for five years, although the company has focused on promoting its own brand name rather than leveraging the IBM name. [273] Lenovo's purchase of IBM's personal computer division was reviewed by the Committee on Foreign Investment in the United States, which allowed the deal to go through, with certain qualifications.[274]

However, Lenovo's success has also been accompanied by controversy. In spring 2006, concerns were raised by members of the U.S.-China Economic and Security Review Commission regarding a planned State Department purchase of 16,000 Lenovo computers, with 900 of the computers intended for use in a classified network connecting U.S. embassies and consulates.[275] Dr. Larry Wortzel, then chairman of the Commission, stated that "[i]f you're a foreign intelligence service and you know that a [U.S.] federal agency is buying… computers from [a Chinese] company, wouldn't you look into the possibility that you could do something about that?"[276] Another Commissioner, Michael Wessel, added that "[t]his event should trigger a broader review of our procurement policies for all our classified networks and communications."[277]

Representative Frank Wolf (R-Va.), then chairman of the House Appropriations Subcommittee on Commerce, Justice, State and the Judiciary, led the effort to address concerns about this issue. In the face of these objections, the State Department indicated that the Lenovo computers would be used only on unclassified networks. In a statement, Representative Wolf said that "I was deeply troubled to learn that the new computers were purchased from a China-based company…. This decision would have had dire consequences for our national security, potentially jeopardizing our investment in a secure IT infrastructure."[278]

For their part, Lenovo company officials have steadfastly denied that there are any reasons to worry about the security of the company's computers. Jeffrey Carlisle, vice president of government relations for Lenovo, stated that the computers would be manufactured in "the same places, using the same processes as I.B.M. had," and that "If anything were detected, it would be a death warrant for the company… No one would ever buy another Lenovo PC. It

[272]Kevin O'Brien, "Lenovo Steps Out Onto Global Stage," *International Herald Tribune*, March 9, 2006. *http://ezproxy.library.nyu.edu:2076/us/lnacademic/results/docview/docview.do?docLinkInd=true&risb=21_T96635569 96&format=GNBFI&sort=RELEVANCE&startDocNo=1&resultsUrlKey=29_T9663556999&cisb=22_T9663556998&tre eMax=true&treeWidth=0&csi=8357&docNo=1.*
[273] Glenn Rifkin and Jenna Smith, "*Quickly Erasing 'I' and 'B' and 'M,'"* New York Times*, April 12, 2006. *http://ezproxy.library.nyu.edu:2076/us/lnacademic/results/docview/docview.do?docLinkInd=true&risb=21_T96639108 91&format=GNBFI&sort=RELEVANCE&startDocNo=1&resultsUrlKey=29_T9663910894&cisb=22_T9663910893&tre eMax=true&treeWidth=0&csi=6742&docNo=5.*
[274] Eric Bangeman, "Uncle Sam Looking Carefully at IBM/Lenovo Deal,*" ArsTechnica* (January 24, 2005). *http://arstechnica.com/old/content/2005/01/4550.ars.*
[275] Grant Gross, "U.S. State Department to Limit Use of Lenovo PCs," *ComputerWorld,* May 19, 2006. *http://www.computerworld.com/s/article/9000639/U.S._State_Department_to_limit_use_of_Lenovo_PCs.*
[276] Eric Bangeman, "Lenovo Laptop Deal Draws Scrutiny from Government Agency," *Ars Technica* (March 26, 2006). *http://arstechnica.com/old/content/2006/03/6475.ars.*
[277] Grant Gross, "U.S. State Department Limits Use of Lenovo PCs," *PC World,* May 19, 2006. *http://www.pcworld.com/article/125802/us_state_department_limits_use_of_lenovo_pcs.html.*
[278] Grant Gross, "U.S. State Department Limits Use of Lenovo PCs," *PC World,* May 19, 2006. *http://www.pcworld.com/article/125802/us_state_department_limits_use_of_lenovo_pcs.html.*

would make no sense to do it."[279] Lenovo Chairman Yang Yuanqing told the Associated Press: "The [Chinese] government isn't involved in any daily operation of the company, including our strategic positions, appointment of our CEO, or our financing…. Our management team is in charge of that. I don't believe because Legend Holdings is our biggest shareholder that this means we are a government-controlled company." [280]

The experience may have left Lenovo executives with a sense that increased engagement with Congressional representatives might head off similar problems in the future, and starting in 2006 Lenovo began to sponsor lobbying efforts on Capitol Hill. From 2006-2009, Lenovo paid a total of $1,060,000 to lobbying firms, engaging the services of Akin Gump Strauss Hauer & Feld; Capstrat; the Gallagher Group; the Duberstein Group; and Miller and Chevalier. The bulk of this amount was paid to Akin Gump Strauss Hauer & Feld: a total of $920,000 for services in 2008-2009, for matters centered on "China" and "technology issues." In addition, Lenovo spent another $2,619,000 in the same period to fund direct lobbying efforts by its own representatives.[281]

MICROCHIP MANUFACTURING
Key Cyber Security and National Security Risks

Recent years have seen increasing attention paid by public officials to the potential security vulnerabilities inherent in the offshoring of computer hardware manufacturing. As was stated in 2008 by Secretary of Homeland Security Michael Chertoff:

> A less often focused on [than cyber espionage] but equally significant threat comes from the supply chain. Increasingly when you buy computers they have components that originate from places all around the world. We need to look at the question of how we assure that people are not embedding in very small components or things that go into computers [things] that can be triggered remotely and then become the basis of ways to [steal] information or [that] could become botnets.[282]

Representatives of private industry have also voiced concerns about the potential for security threats being embedded in computer hardware. As was stated in testimony before the U.S.-China Economic and Security Review Commission by Kevin Coleman, cyber security consultant and senior fellow with the Technolytics Institute:

> Hardware is just as susceptible as software is to hackers through the inclusion of malicious logic….Hidden malicious circuits provide an attacker with a stealthy attack vector. Commercial suppliers are increasingly moving the design, manufacturing, and testing stages of Integrated Circuit (IC) production to a diverse set of countries, which is making the securing of the IC supply chain infeasible. Together, commercial off-the-shelf (COTS) procurement and global production lead to an increasing risk of covert hardware/firmware based cyber attacks. The extraordinary effort required to uncover

---

[279] Steve Lohr, "State Department Yields on PCs from China," *New York Times,* May 23, 2006.
[280] Gregg Keizer, "Lenovo Denies Its PCs Are Security Risk," *ChannelWeb,* May 25, 2006. *http://www.crn.com/security/188500323;jsessionid=3RJWEDHCIPK0DQE1GHRSKHWATMY32JVN?itc=refresh.*
[281] Calculations performed by staff of the U.S.-China Economic and Security Review Commission based on examination of disclosure documents in the U.S. Senate Lobbying Disclosure Act database. Database available at *http://www.senate.gov/legislative//Public_Disclosure/LDA_reports.htm.*
[282] *Popular Mechanics,* "Homeland Chief Chertoff Gives Security Update," October 1, 2009. *http://www.popularmechanics.com/technology/gadgets/4237823.*

such high-tech covert acts, combined with the massive number of chips we would have to test and validate from a circuitry and microcode perspective, as well as the need to scan through tens of millions of lines of code and validate each software instance on billions of devices, come together to make ensuring the integrity of our systems nearly impossible. Security must be designed and built in, not tested for after the fact.[283]

Cyber security expert Jim Gosler[284] has stated that compromised chips and electronics have already been found in DOD systems: "We have found microelectronics and electronics embedded in applications that they shouldn't be there. And it's very clear that a foreign intelligence service put them there."[285]

The Defense Science Board Task Force
2005 Report on High-Performance Microchip Supply

The Department of Defense has taken note of potential security concerns related to the outsourcing of microchip manufacturing. In a report released in early 2005 by the Defense Science Board Task Force on High-Performance Microchip Supply,[286] several statements highlight the dangers of relying on foreign sources for integrated circuit components used in military applications:

"Trustworthiness includes confidence that classified or mission-critical information contained in chip designs is not compromised, reliability is not degraded, and unintended design elements are not inserted in chips as a result of design or fabrication in conditions open to adversary agents."[287]

"Defense system electronic hardware, like that used in commercial applications, has undergone a radical transformation. Whereas custom circuits, unique to specific applications, were once widely used, most information processing today is performed by combinations of memory chips (DRAMs, SRAMs, etc.) which store data (including programs), and programmable microchips, such as Structured ASICs [application-specific integrated circuits], Programmable Logic Arrays (PLAs), central processors (CPUs), and digital signal processors (DSPs), which operate on the data. Of the two classes of parts, the latter have more intricate designs, which make them difficult to validate (especially after manufacturing) and thus more subject to undetected compromise."[288]

---

[283] U.S.-China Economic and Security Review Commission, *Hearing on China's Propaganda and Influence Operations, Its Intelligence Activities that Target the United States, and the Resulting Impacts on U.S. National Security*, testimony of Kevin Coleman, April 30, 2009.

[284] Jim Gosler is or has been a Sandia fellow, National Security Agency visiting scientist, and the founding director of the Central Intelligence Agency's Clandestine Information Technology Office. See The White House, "The United States Cyber Challenge," May 8, 2009. *http://www.whitehouse.gov/files/documents/cyber/The%20United%20States%20Cyber%20Challenge%201.1%20%28updated%205-8-09%29.pdf.*

[285] CBS News, *60 Minutes*, "Cyber War: Sabotaging the System," November 8, 2009. *http://www.cbsnews.com/stories/2009/11/06/60minutes/main5555565.shtml.*

[286] Department of Defense, *Report of the Defense Science Board Task Force on High-Performance Microchips Supply* (Arlington, VA: Office of the Under Secretary of Defense for Acquisition, Technology, and Logistics, February 2005). *http://www.acq.osd.mil/dsb/reports/ADA435563.pdf.*

[287] Department of Defense, *Report of the Defense Science Board Task Force on High-Performance Microchips Supply* (Arlington, VA: Office of the Under Secretary of Defense for Acquisition, Technology, and Logistics, February 2005), p. 17. *http://www.acq.osd.mil/dsb/reports/ADA435563.pdf.*

[288] Department of Defense, *Report of the Defense Science Board Task Force on High-Performance Microchips Supply* (Arlington, VA: Office of the Under Secretary of Defense for Acquisition, Technology, and Logistics, February 2005), pp. 44-45. *http://www.acq.osd.mil/dsb/reports/ADA435563.pdf.*

> *"The semiconductor world can be divided into two broad producer segments – standard (commodity) and custom products. Standard products are sold to many customers for use in many applications; custom products – ASICs – are designed, manufactured and sold to one customer for specific uses. The economic models for suppliers and customers in these two segments are very different. While a great deal of attention is paid to securing trusted ASIC supplies for the DOD community, questions must also be asked about the future sources of standard commercial products."[289]*
>
> *"Since it is clear that the general tendency is to manufacture leading-edge semiconductor products outside the United States and the fixed costs of ASIC design and fabrication are skyrocketing, a clear trend is emerging for designers to use as few custom semiconductor products as possible; instead, they employ programmable standard products. Semiconductor standard products are those whose functionality can be changed by software programming, as in the case of microprocessors (MPUs) and digital signal processors (DSPs), or hardware programmability, as in the case of field programmable products such as field programmable gate arrays. While these standard products will also increasingly be manufactured offshore, their functionality is mostly controlled by the user, [thus] it may be impossible to independently secure that functionality."[290]*
>
> *"Programmable parts have more intricate designs, which make them difficult to validate (especially after manufacturing) and thus more subject to undetected compromise. Thus, it is important that programmable components be "trustable," though only to a degree that is commensurate with their application."[291]*
>
> *"Trustworthiness of custom and commercial systems that support military operations – and the advances in microchip technology underlying our information superiority… ha[ve] been jeopardized. <u>Trust cannot be added to integrated circuits after fabrication; electrical testing and reverse engineering cannot be relied upon to detect undesired alterations in military integrated circuits</u>"* (emphasis in original).[292]

The production and manufacture of customized microchips such as application-specific integrated circuits (ASICs) is a complex process involving three phases: design, mask making, and fabrication. Each phase presents opportunities for an adversary to insert vulnerabilities that can render a device useless upon activation of a "kill" switch or change the functionality in a way that reduces security by leaking or corrupting sensitive data. Since a single device may contain millions of transistors, the ability to identify malicious circuits is almost impossible to accomplish either practically or economically.

---

[289] Department of Defense, *Report of the Defense Science Board Task Force on High-Performance Microchips Supply* (Arlington, VA: Office of the Under Secretary of Defense for Acquisition, Technology, and Logistics, February 2005), p. 39. *http://www.acq.osd.mil/dsb/reports/ADA435563.pdf.*

[290] Department of Defense, *Report of the Defense Science Board Task Force on High-Performance Microchips Supply* (Arlington, VA: Office of the Under Secretary of Defense for Acquisition, Technology, and Logistics, February 2005), p. 40. *http://www.acq.osd.mil/dsb/reports/ADA435563.pdf.*

[291] Department of Defense, *Report of the Defense Science Board Task Force on High-Performance Microchips Supply* (Arlington, VA: Office of the Under Secretary of Defense for Acquisition, Technology, and Logistics, February 2005), p. 40. *http://www.acq.osd.mil/dsb/reports/ADA435563.pdf.*

[292] Department of Defense, *Report of the Defense Science Board Task Force on High-Performance Microchips Supply* (Arlington, VA: Office of the Under Secretary of Defense for Acquisition, Technology, and Logistics, February 2005), p. 3. *http://www.acq.osd.mil/dsb/reports/ADA435563.pdf.*

During the design phase, engineers have direct access to the design database and can, if they so desire, make subtle changes that modify the functionality or insert malicious code such as kill switches, Trojan horses, worms, or many other backdoor features. During the masking phase, ultraviolet (UV) light is used to expose patterns on the layers of the microprocessor in a process similar to photography. Masks used for the chip-making process are called stencils. When these are used with UV light, they create various patterns on each layer of the microprocessor. Similar to the design phase, the masking phase offers a potential malicious actor the opportunity to change the design of the circuit by substituting one mask for another. Changing the mask allows the addition of transistors that can alter functionality or insert malicious code.

The fabrication phase is the final step in the production of ASICs. During manufacture, it is possible to make changes to the design or embed hundreds of additional transistors into each circuit with little probability of being detected. It is also possible to alter the functionality of an integrated circuit after manufacture by using a focused-ion-beam (FIB) etching machine to remove material from the chip and etch new connections between the transistors. While this is a legitimate process for modifying chip design, it can also be used for nefarious purposes in the hands of a skilled technician. This technology can be particularly useful to those wanting to disrupt U.S. systems by focusing on the maintenance and repair chain following the initial production of microchips.

Recent Cases Involving Counterfeited Computer Equipment from China

Over the past several years there have been a number of law enforcement cases involving counterfeit computer chips of Chinese origin that were sold to U.S. government agencies. Such cases raise concerns for the potential security risk of tampering. However, they also raise concerns of a more prosaic but still serious nature, such as the risk of defective components being installed in critical computer, communications, or weapons systems. Many of these cases have involved the counterfeiting of computer products produced and marketed by Cisco Systems, Inc. Three such examples are the following:

1.   In January 2008, Michael and Robert Edman were charged with conspiring with a contact in China to purchase computer equipment and then falsely relabeling and selling the items as Cisco products. Operating under the company name Syren Technology, the two brothers allegedly shipped the counterfeit Cisco products directly to customers, including "the Marine Corps, Air Force, FBI [Federal Bureau of Investigation], Federal Aviation Administration, Department of Energy, as well as defense contractors, universities, school districts and financial institutions." The men entered a partial guilty plea to the charges in September 2009.[293]

2.   In January 2010, Yongcai Li, a Chinese citizen, was sentenced in California to 30 months in prison and ordered to pay $790,683 in restitution to Cisco Systems following from a conviction for trafficking in counterfeit Cisco computer products. Working through his company Gaoyi Technology, located in Shenzhen, China. Mr. Li procured counterfeit Cisco products in China and then shipped the products to the United States.[294]

---

[293] U.S. Attorney's Office for the Southern District of Texas Press Release, "Brothers Plead Guilty to Selling Counterfeit Cisco Products to Bureau of Prisons," September 9, 2009. _http://www.justice.gov/criminal/cybercrime/edmanPlea.pdf._

294 U.S. Department of Justice Press Release, "Departments of Justice and Homeland Security Announce 30 Convictions, More Than $143 Million in Seizures from Initiative Targeting Traffickers in Counterfeit Network Hardware," May 6, 2010. _http://www.fbi.gov/pressrel/pressrel10/convictions_050610.htm_.

3. Also in January 2010, Ehab Ashoor, 49, a Saudi citizen, was sentenced in Texas to 51 months in prison and ordered to pay $119,400 in restitution to Cisco Systems. A federal jury found Mr. Ashoor guilty of charges related to trafficking in counterfeit Cisco products. Although no specific security threat is alleged, a Department of Justice press release sounded a note of alarm about the case, noting that "Ashoor purchased counterfeit Cisco Gigabit Interface Converters (GBICs) from an online vendor in China with the intention of selling them to the U.S. Department of Defense for use by U.S. Marine Corps personnel operating in Iraq," to be used on a computer network "used by the U.S. Marine Corps to transmit troop movements [and] relay intelligence."[295]

Many such investigations into counterfeit computer equipment were conducted by federal authorities under the names of "Operation Cisco Raider" and "Operation Network Raider." According to a Department of Justice statement made in May 2010:

"To date, [Immigration and Customs Enforcement--ICE] agents have seized counterfeit Cisco products having an estimated retail value of more than $35 million. ICE investigations have led to eight indictments and felony convictions... [Customs and Border Patrol--CBP] has made 537 seizures of counterfeit Cisco network hardware since 2005, and 47 seizures of Cisco labels for counterfeit products. In total, ICE and CBP seized more than 94,000 counterfeit Cisco network components and labels with a total estimated retail value of more than $86 million during the course of the operation."[296]

However, the Department of Justice statement immediately above did not clearly indicate to what extent these counterfeit computer components originated in China and/or how many of the arrests and convictions involved linkages to China. Public statements from the Department of Justice have not alleged any negative actions by the Chinese government and have stressed the cooperative nature of these investigations with PRC officials: A Federal Bureau of Investigation (FBI) spokeswoman stated in May 2008 that the bureau "worked very closely with the Chinese government" on such cases,[297] and a May 2010 press release stated that "U.S. law enforcement authorities continue to work with China's Ministry of Public Security (MPS) to combat the manufacture and export of counterfeit network hardware from China... This ongoing work is being facilitated by the [Intellectual Property] Criminal Enforcement Working Group of the U.S.-China Joint Liaison Group for law enforcement, which is co-chaired by the Criminal Division [of the FBI] and the MPS."[298]

TESTING OF INTEGRATED CIRCUITS

Testing of integrated circuits to ensure the integrity of batches and manufacturing processes dealing with physical consistency, authenticity, and materials integrity can be partially done using electric current testing and layer scanning methods currently in industry use. However,

---

[295] U.S. Department of Justice Press Release, "Departments of Justice and Homeland Security Announce 30 Convictions, More Than $143 Million in Seizures from Initiative Targeting Traffickers in Counterfeit Network Hardware," May 6, 2010. *http://www.fbi.gov/pressrel/pressrel10/convictions_050610.htm.*

[296] U.S. Department of Justice Press Release, Departments of Justice and Homeland Security Announce 30 Convictions, More Than $143 Million in Seizures from Initiative Targeting Traffickers in Counterfeit Network Hardware," May 6, 2010. *http://www.fbi.gov/pressrel/pressrel10/convictions_050610.htm.*

[297] John Markoff, "FBI Says the Military Had Bogus Computer Gear," *New York Times,* May 9, 2008.

[298] U.S. Department of Justice Press Release, Departments of Justice and Homeland Security Announce 30 Convictions, More Than $143 Million in Seizures from Initiative Targeting Traffickers in Counterfeit Network Hardware," May 6, 2010. *http://www.fbi.gov/pressrel/pressrel10/convictions_050610.htm.*

exhaustive preventative testing of the deeply embedded purposes of designs within an integrated circuit is increasingly less possible as densities approach and increase below 20 nanometers. As stated in a March 2008 article from the online journal of the Institute of Electrical and Electronics Engineers:

- *Although commercial chip makers routinely and exhaustively test chips with hundreds of millions of logic gates, they can't afford to inspect everything. So instead they focus on how well the chip performs specific functions. For a microprocessor destined for use in a cell phone, for instance, the chip maker will check to see whether all the phone's various functions work. Any extraneous circuitry that doesn't interfere with the chip's normal functions won't show up in these tests…Nor can chip makers afford to test every chip. From a batch of thousands, technicians select a single chip for physical inspection, assuming that the manufacturing process has yielded essentially identical devices. They then laboriously grind away a thin layer of the chip, put the chip into a scanning electron microscope, and then take a picture of it, repeating the process until every layer of the chip has been imaged. Even here, spotting a tiny discrepancy amid a chip's many layers and millions or billions of transistors is a fantastically difficult task, and the chip is destroyed in the process.[299]*

- *A single plane like the DOD's next generation F-35 Joint Strike Fighter can contain an 'insane number' of chips, says one semiconductor expert familiar with that aircraft's design.[300] Estimates from other sources put the total at several hundred to more than a thousand. And tracing a part back to its source is not always straightforward. The dwindling of domestic chip and electronics manufacturing in the United States, combined with the phenomenal growth of suppliers in countries like China, has only deepened the U.S. military's concern.[301]*

- *Recognizing this enormous vulnerability, the DOD recently launched its most ambitious program yet to verify the integrity of the electronics that will underpin future additions to its arsenal. In December, the Defense Advanced Research Projects Agency (DARPA), the Pentagon's R&D wing, released details about a three-year initiative it calls the Trust in Integrated Circuits program. The findings from the program could give the military-- and defense contractors who make sensitive microelectronics like the weapons systems for the F-35--a guaranteed method of determining whether their chips have been compromised.[302]*

Even if the military establishment is successful in determining which chips have been compromised in its microelectronics systems, problems with microchips and integrated circuits have the potential to cause significant harm to the entire country through disruptions of nonmilitary systems such as power plants, telephone systems, air traffic control infrastructure, Internet services, and private/public networks. Many, if not all, of these systems will continue to rely on nontrusted sources for technology products and services.

---

[299] Sally Adee, "The Hunt for the Kill Switch," *IEEE (Institute of Electrical and Electronics Engineers) Spectrum* (May 2008). *http://www. spectrum.ieee.org/semiconductors/design/the-hunt-for-the-kill-switch*.

[300] Sally Adee, "The Hunt for the Kill Switch," *IEEE (Institute of Electrical and Electronics Engineers) Spectrum* (May 2008). *http://www. spectrum.ieee.org/semiconductors/design/the-hunt-for-the-kill-switch*.

[301] Sally Adee, "The Hunt for the Kill Switch," *IEEE (Institute of Electrical and Electronics Engineers) Spectrum* (May 2008). *http://www. spectrum.ieee.org/semiconductors/design/the-hunt-for-the-kill-switch*.

[302] Sally Adee, "The Hunt for the Kill Switch," *IEEE* (Institute of Electrical and Electronics Engineers) *Spectrum* (May 2008*). http://www. spectrum.ieee.org/semiconductors/design/the-hunt-for-the-kill-switch*.

Kill Switches and Backdoors

Although a sufficient reserve of trusted critical computer chips for a weapon system such as the F-35 can be identified and stockpiled, this is not the case with more commoditized telecommunications systems and components. The most-expected tampering threats in fabricating integrated circuits are generally assumed to be the inclusion of kill switches or backdoors. Each is defined as follows:

> A kill switch is any manipulation of the chip's software or hardware that would cause the chip to die outright... A backdoor, by contrast, lets outsiders gain access to the system through code or hardware to disable or enable a specific function. Because this method works without shutting down the whole chip, users remain unaware of the intrusion. An enemy could use it to bypass battlefield radio encryption, for instance.[303]

Most computer users today are well aware of the risks in downloading computer viruses through software vulnerabilities, but few consider the dangers of purchasing a computer or other network devices with security risks already etched into the silicon used to make the microchips. As an example, encryption in today's systems is often done through integrated circuits dedicated to this function.

> It is possible to add a code during the manufacture of the integrated circuit that will disable the encryption function when the code is received from an outside source. The circuit could also be altered through the addition of transistors that will disable encryption at a set time. Not knowing that encryption has been disabled, the user could continue to send sensitive or classified messages that would be readable by a hacker representing a hostile nation or a criminal enterprise.[304]

Flash memory could be added to networked printers that result in saving image files of every document printed and forwarding those images to a third party. Kill switches could be embedded into DOD systems to bring the systems down at a predetermined time or upon receipt of external instructions or codes. The potential for harm is enormous, extending from simple identity theft by criminal enterprises to disrupting networks and defense systems vital to national security.

---

[303] Sally Adee, "The Hunt for the Kill Switch," *IEEE* (Institute of Electrical and Electronics Engineers) *Spectrum* (May 2008). *http://www. spectrum.ieee.org/semiconductors/design/the-hunt-for-the-kill-switch.*
[304] Sally Adee, "The Hunt for the Kill Switch," *IEEE* (Institute of Electrical and Electronics Engineers) *Spectrum* (May 2008). *http://www. spectrum.ieee.org/semiconductors/design/the-hunt-for-the-kill-switch.*

CONCLUSIONS & RECOMMENDATIONS

SUPPLY CHAIN SECURITY AND POTENTIAL IMPACTS ON GOVERNMENT CONTRACTING FOR SENSITIVE SYSTEMS

The discussion of market segments and products discussed previously in this report demonstrates how enormously intertwined are the technology supply chains between the United States and China in the communications market and how varied the considerations are when assessing the relevant issues and impacts. An ever-growing multitude of components (hundreds of thousands, or perhaps millions) now constitute an integrated U.S. supply chain supporting communications and information exchanges on a global basis.

Analysis of China's technology integration is not so different from the analysis of the trade dynamics of any international resource: tracing trade routes, purchases, and ports of call reveals a great deal of information, some of which may be useful evidence in forming conclusions about source-derived risks. In technology, networks constitute global information "trade routes," with switches, routers, hubs, handsets, and computers becoming the ports of call. Numerous foreign manufacturers contribute to the supply chain in the U.S. communications sector. If foreign suppliers do not already provide the majority of products in these trade routes (either directly under their own brand names or indirectly under U.S. brand names), it is only a matter of time for this to become true if present trends continue.[305]

Diligent analysis of communications supply chains, such as switches, routers, modems, handsets, LANS, WANs, etc., reveals very few areas where supply chains did not have at least some integration with Chinese manufacturers as well as manufacturers from many other global points of origin. This is due in great part to sourcing strategies adopted by U.S. manufacturers and service providers. Outsourcing is one of the key ways in which U.S. product manufacturers have been able to achieve greater efficiencies in their business models, satisfying shareholder demands for ever-increasing profits and consumer demands for ever-improving value-to-price ratios.

However, as the extent of manufacturing outsourcing increases, the abilities of a nation to mitigate risks in its high-technology supply chain are further eroded. High-technology risks have accelerated in parallel with the dramatic development of telecommunications and information technologies. Vulnerabilities in the communications supply chain have the potential to be enormous given the complex number of manufacturers, mergers, acquisitions, and general globalization of the technology supply chain. A network architecture, whether in space or on the ground, might have thousands of suppliers and hundreds of thousands of subcomponents.

In many cases, U.S. government tracing of products or components to points of origin often consists of looking at product lines and "country of origin" based on 50 percent cost and point of "manufacture" rules (such as in the Buy America Act, or substantial transformation rules such as those found in the Trade Agreements Act).[306] Although components and subcomponents may be made in other countries, they may still be eligible to be sold as completed domestic products in the United States. Hypothetically, a U.S. buyer may not realize that a product designated as domestic under Buy America and Trade Agreements Act rules, and purchased from a domestic

---

[305] Reperi internal research on trends in the global communications supply chain.
[306] Reed Smith LLP, "New Amendment Rationalizes Country-of-Origin Preferences for Defense and Civilian Acquisitions," Client Bulletin 03-03, January 2003. *http://www.reedsmith.com/_db/_documents/bull0303.pdf.*

U.S. company, may still be partly or largely sourced from an overseas supplier. A meaningful attempt to trace product or component origins in the telecommunications and technology supply chains would be a monumental undertaking, requiring extraordinary levels of interaction and cooperation with both foreign and domestic businesses.

Using the U.S. Department of Defense as an example, tracing product origins adds layers of new complexity to an already complex supply chain environment. In a 2004 estimate, the Department of Defense maintained an inventory of supplies and equipment worth more than $80 billion across multiple services and organizations, many of which use different automated supply systems.[307] Simply unifying and streamlining inventory management systems and methods is a difficult task that may take years to succeed, even without adding checks and balances based on considerations of electronic and information security risks based on product or component country of origin. In many cases, government procurement officials simply rely on established standard practices and do not examine products to a fine enough level to be meaningful for determining countries of origin at component levels.

According to the Defense Science Board Task Force, "The Defense Department does not directly acquire components at the integrated circuit level. Individual circuits are most often specified by designers of subsystems; even system primes have little knowledge of the sources of the components used in their system level products."[308] This is a particularly important point when considering government options: How will a government buyer know what it is procuring within the context of foreign supplier security risks at the integrated circuit level, if the prime manufacturer from whom they are purchasing does not know what it is selling?

RESPONSES TO SUPPLY CHAIN CHALLENGES

Shaping the rate of change of supply chains and technologies will be a major challenge of the 21st century. We may have to cope both with technological change happening too fast (the tempo of technological developments producing new risks faster than the rate of effective response) or too slow (the tempo of innovation no longer being competitive). Are there ways constructively to change either the pace of technological change or the willingness of the U.S. market to be meaningfully selective in deciding which new technologies should be developed and adopted? Where supply chains are transforming too quickly or too slowly, how may their rate of change be influenced beneficially?

Government buyers and commercial providers must develop both a keener sense of component-level make-ups and capabilities/risks of telecom and technology products being sold to the U.S. government, and work together to mitigate or limit risks. U.S. government organizations must also become adept at tracking the dynamics of the global telecom and technology markets, to include maintaining a watchful eye on mergers, acquisitions, technology trends, and other business context changes that may have profound strategic meaning for government business.

---

[307] Daniel W. Engels et al., "Improving Visibility in the DOD Supply Chain," http://www.almc.army.mil/alog/issues/mayJun04/alog_supple%20chain.htm.
[308] Office of the Under Secretary of Defense for Acquisition, Technology, and Logistics, *Report of the Defense Science Board Task Force on High-Performance Microchip Supply* (Arlington, VA: Department of Defense, February 2005), p. 5. http://www.acq.osd.mil/dsb/reports/ADA435563.pdf.

In trying to determine the acceptability of risks resulting from further Chinese involvement in vital U.S. supply chains, issues such as Collingridge's "control dilemma" complicate the decision-making process.[309] That is to say, by locking in a technologically exclusionary policy too soon, the United States may irrevocably harm its own global competitiveness; However, delaying decision-making long enough to better understand the potential risks involved may result in limited options and lost opportunities, or in the worst cases, irrevocable harm if catastrophic consequences occur.

Globally, innovation in the communications industry is not uniform, unilateral, or symmetric, but it is rapid. The changing nature of innovation and sourcing is another conundrum that decision makers must wrestle with: how can policy frameworks account for the continuous nature of technological evolution and the vast and ever-evolving array of options for obtaining or providing new communications technologies? New thinking and a pluralistic institutional approach is called for that will provide appropriate mechanisms to:

- monitor new Chinese technologies and supply-chain risks to provide meaningful early warnings of unacceptable risks;
- spur American technological and supply-chain innovations that will enable means for responding to early warnings or mitigating the impacts of such risks when early warning surveillance fails; and
- provide effective implementation for appropriate technological or supply-chain responses, when such actions are warranted.

The rapid pace of change in the communications market, the profound impacts of these continual changes, and the way in which individual market segments play into the overall communications supply chain all warrant continual surveillance. How the U.S. government (and commercial vendors used by the government) may suffer from increased national security risk exposure, the erosion of the national industrial base, and other potential future liabilities and outcomes must be reassessed on an ongoing basis.

THE CHESS GAME OF STANDARDS –
The New Method for Owning Supply Chains

Large parts of the supply chain have gone to China – a transfer brought about by business evolution rather than revolution, with China filling a void created by a manufacturing base in America that, for many products, has been globally less competitive on a per-unit cost production basis. In many ways, China's presence in the U.S. supply chain has fulfilled vital needs of American companies and has been a "good marriage" for many. By all indications, Chinese companies have gone to considerable lengths to earn a seat among global technology giants such as IBM, Alcatel-Lucent, and other respected companies. On current growth paths, companies like Huawei should overtake the largest technology companies in the world. This is not surprising when we acknowledge that companies like Huawei have gone to great lengths to identify, understand, and emulate the most successful global business models they encounter.

---

[309]David Collingridge, "The Social Control of Technology," (Birmingham, England: University of Aston, Technology Policy Unit, 1980). The fundamental dilemma of technological governance is that, during early manifestations of technological evolution, there are many paths for advancement that may seem appropriate, but not enough is known to allow choosing the best paths forward. By the time enough is known about the impacts of a technological evolution for best paths to become apparent, society is already locked in, has vested its interests, and is left with limited options.

U.S. businesses looking to reduce labor costs have increasingly moved parts of their production chain to China. Initially, this involved preprocessing of raw materials and basic manufacturing to reduce costs and make companies more competitive. Over the years, this process has expanded to include much of the product development, design, and production cycles and is an expanding phenomenon fueled by circumstances within both the United States and China. Creating a technology product, such as a cell phone, or wireless broadband equipment like WiMAX (a standard much like the WiFi routers in our homes and offices – only designed to cover miles of distance) requires numerous manufacturers of all of the parts to agree on how those pieces are going to interoperate or work together. Numerous working groups exist to create standards so that wireless networks can operate on frequencies that are different in each country.

Eventually, standards are adopted and thousands of product parts are made to support that standard; for example, 3Com must design routers for wireless Internet protocols. For devices to talk to each other in the United States or globally, international bodies must agree on the standard that 3Com will use to guide its design process. Because the United States has been the technology leader of the world, most standards have been influenced by North American companies such as IBM, Intel, Cisco, 3Com, Qualcomm, Microsoft, Nortel, and Motorola. However, this is changing: In 2007, Intel received approval to perform chip manufacturing in China and is investing in research and development and production with Chinese manufacturers. This move was necessary to compete with Advanced Micro Devices and other manufacturers. As more products are manufactured overseas, supply chains have followed. In the wireless market, routers, cell phones, power supplies, peripherals, software, control devices, and semiconductors are produced in China. With China's ready supply of design engineers, innovative Chinese companies have spawned new, unique products.

Throwing a population of more than 1.5 billion potential consumers at the wireless market, then adding manufacturing for North America, South America, and Europe to the equation, gives China the ability to dominate standards--in other words, determine product specifications for next-generation products. In the communications world, that means the protocols for how networks will communicate will likely be heavily influenced by China, and manufacturers outside of the China market may begin to lose global market share in dramatic fashion.

INNOVATION IN AMERICA, AND THE SHORTAGE OF MATHEMATICIANS, SCIENTISTS, AND ENGINEERS

The Thomson Reuters' *2008 Global Innovation Study* showed that on the basis of the total number of unique inventions issued in granted patents and published patent applications, 70 percent of the top ten innovators in the United States were non-U.S. companies. Meanwhile, U.S. companies are conspicuously absent from Asian and European top ten lists. [310] When we further examine the surge of patent filings in China (the number of patent filings is one of the classic indicators of the levels of innovation in a country), as of 2007 China was well ahead of the United States in the number of filings annually and may soon overtake the United States in the number of patents issued annually. Based on 2006 statistics, patent filings in China were

---

[310] Thomson Reuters, *2008 Global Innovation Study*, March 24, 2009. http://science.thomsonreuters.com/press/2009/innovation_study/.

increasing at a rate of 20 percent per year, with Huawei Technologies standing as the single largest filer of 20-year patents.[311]

This comparative view offers an indication that innovation in China may be outpacing innovation in the United States and that the patent-seeking environment for multinational and U.S. entities is now dramatically more complicated. Earlier patent filings in China may represent prior arts[312] to a later patent filing in the United States. With China also offering ten-year intermediate patents ("utility model") that do not require the same robust level of effort and proofs that are necessary to obtain a full-fledged 20-year invention patent (comparable intermediate patents are not available in the United States), American innovators may find themselves at a profound disadvantage in seeking intellectual property protections.

While the manufacturing supply chain has shifted to Chinese and overseas markets for a range of communications products, so have design and engineering. For America to remain competitive and generate future innovations, as well as to maintain control over technology standards, it is essential to provide incentives for continued development of the U.S. scientific and engineering workforce. Such an effort cannot be modest. It must be a commitment on a grand scale in order to reverse course and regain headway. Such measures would be akin to developing public-private partnerships that shift program dollars into funding tuition for math, science, and engineering.

Outsourcing the control of manufacturing and manufacturing processes also has the unintended consequence of making domestic revival of those processes more difficult. If a U.S. enterprise attempts to bring back some outsourced activities – even in an effort to reduce potential vulnerabilities – it may find that the necessary capabilities are difficult to reconstitute, due not just to a loss of physical plant facilities but also to an erosion in relevant skills among the workforce.[313] Outsourcing can also affect future prospects for technological innovation: As the outsourcing trend continues, it has already been shown that the number of students enrolling in engineering and computer science disciplines in the United States has been declining for several years. This trend will continue as long as the potential job market and pay structures offer fewer job opportunities. Talent will shift to where the leading-edge research and development is taking place.

The figure below illustrates how the loss of science and engineering graduates in America continues to contribute to this problem.

---

[311]Michael Orey, "Patent Filings Surge in China," *Bloomberg Businessweek*, June 3, 2008. *http://www.businessweek.com/bwdaily/dnflash/content/jun2008/db2008063_332712.htm?chan=top+news_top+news +index_technology*.

[312] In patent law, "prior art" is "all information that has been made available to the public in any form before a given date that might be relevant to a patent's claims of originality... If an invention has been described in prior art, a patent on that invention is not valid." See Wikipedia, "Prior Art." *http://en.wikipedia.org/wiki/Prior_art.*

[313] Reperi – General knowledge based on experience. Also, *http://www.engtrends.com/IEE/1005E.php*. Computer science and engineering saw declining student interest in the early 2000s. Relative undergraduate enrollments ("computer" fraction of engineering) began to decline in the late 1990s, and total undergraduate enrollments began to decline in the early 2000s. Data now show that graduate enrollments are being affected.

Table 3: Computer Science and Engineering Bachelor's Degree Enrollments in the United States, 1980-2005

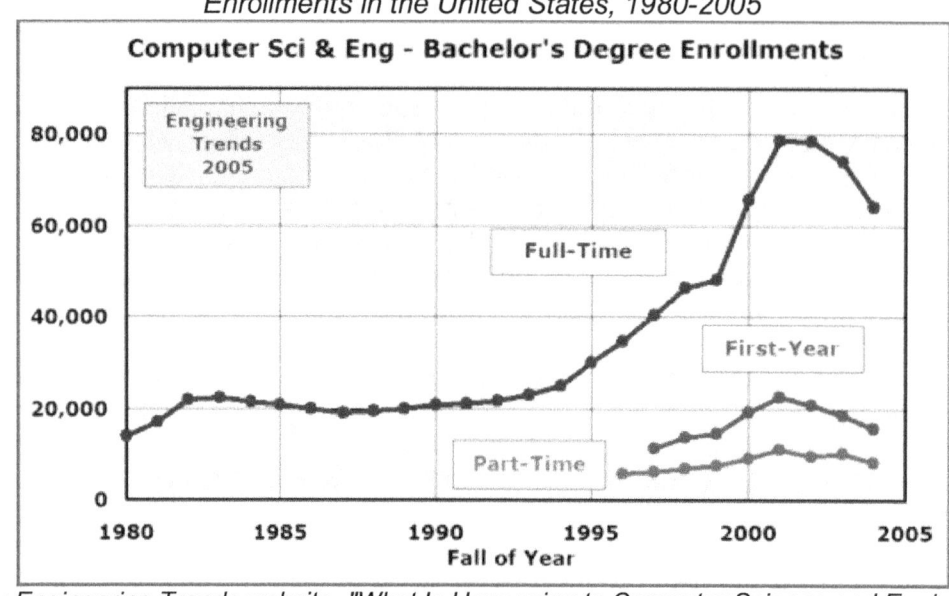

Source: Engineering Trends website, "What Is Happening to Computer Science and Engineering?" Report 1005E, October 2005. http://www.engtrends.com/IEE/1005E.php.

Without necessary talent and processes in place, the United States could find itself at a disadvantage in dealing with foreign suppliers who may or may not be willing to supply the resources needed during a national emergency. Incentives are needed to stimulate development of next-generation technology solutions as well as alternatives that reduce dependency on foreign manufacturers. Developing such alternatives will require investment and the funding of continued technological innovation.

PRODUCT CONTROL ISSUES IN GOVERNMENT COMMUNICATIONS SYSTEMS

The government should develop vulnerabilities models for assessing present and future supply chain vulnerabilities and their impacts on national security and network security, in tandem with supply chain testing of individual components. When risks are well quantified, reasonable actions should be taken to address any unacceptable impacts in the telecommunications and communications sector. This must be done particularly with an eye toward protecting critical elements of the defense industrial base and secure critical communications infrastructure. Such steps might include the following:

- Developing incentives for returning critical vulnerable supply chain elements back to the United States for manufacturing by U.S. companies.
- Asking vendors, in acquiring commercial network services from commercial providers, to inventory and certify vital networks to the component and individual component level, identifying which subelements were manufactured by foreign manufacturers either inside or outside of the United States, regardless of brand identity.
- Eliminating or reducing the number of non-U.S. vendors who receive government funds for contracting and/or subcontracting work on sensitive systems. (This has been difficult to accomplish, primarily due to the global nature of manufacturing and resource

acquisitions, as well as to government pressures to reduce costs. Turning the situation around and moving against the stream will cost ever more as time progresses and be ever more difficult to implement.)

In gaining a broad and deep view of the infusion of outsourced technologies and products, we see signs of momentum that are potentially irresistible. The American economy must learn how to thrive in the avalanche zone of the global telecom and technology marketplaces. America must learn to emphasize and export those areas of business where America offers a better value, and efficiently and safely import in those areas where America does not offer better value.

It will be important to observe China's strategic investments in technology throughout the communications supply chain. An appropriate, multifaceted approach would include a review of each layer of the supply chain based upon historical facts covering mergers and acquisitions, technology architectures, technology evolutions, and supply chain consolidations. Without being unduly alarmist, decision makers in both government and industry should nevertheless take an objective look at the potential security vulnerabilities posed by dependence upon Chinese corporations for electronics components and/or telecommunications services and work toward solutions that appropriately balance U.S. economic and national security interests.

APPENDIX A
WHAT IS A CYBER ATTACK?

Most personal computers are now networked and have access to other systems throughout the Internet and/or private networks managed or leased by government agencies and business enterprises. The ready linkages between personal computers have facilitated the spread of malicious code often referred to as viruses or malware. (The term "computer virus" is sometimes used as a catch-all phrase to include all types of malware, including computer viruses, worms, Trojan horses, most rootkits, backdoors, botnets, and other malicious and unwanted software, including true viruses.[314])

Network services such as the Internet; e-mail; instant messaging; and file-sharing systems, such as social networking sites, can all be used to propagate malware. It is easy to load malware to a system from a compact disk, USB (universal serial bus) storage device, or many similar means. Furthermore, new devices and external links are constantly introduced to wire-line and wireless networking environments. We live in a networked world, and almost every device accessing those networks can pose a potential cyber security risk.

Antivirus software is used to prevent, detect, and remove malware, including computer viruses, worms, and Trojan horses. A variety of strategies are typically employed to thwart malware. Signature-based detection involves searching for known malicious patterns in executable code. However, it is possible for a user to be infected with new malware for which no remedy yet exists. To counter such "zero-day" threats, heuristics (a *heuristic* is a mental shortcut that allows people to solve problems and make judgments quickly and efficiently) can be used. One type of heuristic approach, generic signatures, can identify new viruses or variants of existing viruses by looking for known malicious code (or slight variations of such code) in files. Some antivirus software can also predict what a file will do if opened/run by emulating it in a sandbox (a "firewalled" application space that allows an operating system to safely run a program as a test, to see if it might be hostile before allowing it to run in the system's main memory space) and analyzing what it does to see if it performs any malicious actions. If it does, this could mean that the file is malicious.[315]

Unlike other exploits, distributed denial of service (DDOS) attacks are not used to gain unauthorized access or control of a system; instead, they are designed to render the system unusable. One common method of attack involves saturating the target (victim) machine with external communications requests such that it cannot respond to legitimate traffic or responds

---

[314] A computer virus is a computer program that can copy itself and infect a computer without the permission or knowledge of the owner. A computer worm is a self-replicating computer program. It uses a network to send copies of itself to other computers on the network, and it may do so without any user intervention. A Trojan horse is a program that disguises itself as another program. Similar to viruses, these programs are hidden and usually cause an unwanted effect, such as installing a backdoor into the system that can be used by hackers. Rootkits allow the concealment of a malicious program that is installed on a system by modifying the host operating system so that the malware is hidden from the user. Rootkits can prevent a malicious process from being visible in the system's list of processes or keep its files from being read. A backdoor is a method of bypassing normal authentication procedures. Once a system has been compromised (by one of the above methods or in some other way), one or more backdoors may be installed. Backdoors may also be installed prior to malicious software, to allow attackers entry. In order to coordinate the activity of many infected computers, attackers have used coordinating systems known as botnets. In a botnet, the malware allows the attacker to give instructions to all the infected systems simultaneously. Botnets can also be used to push upgraded malware to the infected systems, keeping them resistant to antivirus software or other security measures.

[315] Peter Szor, *The Art of Computer Virus Research and Defense,*(Addison-Wesley, 2005), pp. 474–481.

so slowly as to be rendered effectively unavailable. In general terms, DDOS attacks are implemented by either forcing the targeted computer(s) to reset, consuming its resources so that it can no longer provide its intended service, or obstructing the communication media between the intended users and the victim so that they can no longer communicate adequately.[316]

On two occasions to date, attackers have performed domain name server (DNS) backbone distributed denial of service attacks on the overall Internet DNS root servers. Since this class of DNS provides baseline DNS service to the entire Internet, these two DDOS attacks might be classified as attempts to take down the entire Internet; however, it is unclear what the attackers' true motivations were. The first occurred in October 2002 and disrupted service at nine of the 13 root servers. The second occurred in February 2007 and caused disruptions at two of the root servers.[317]

In the weeks leading up to the five-day 2008 South Ossetia war, a DDOS attack directed at Georgian government sites containing the message "win+love+in+Rusia" effectively overloaded and shut down multiple Georgian servers. Websites targeted included the website of the Georgian president, Mikhail Saakashvili, (which was rendered inoperable for 24 hours), and the National Bank of Georgia. The Russian government was widely suspected of orchestrating the attack through a proxy, the St. Petersburg-based criminal gang known as the Russian Business Network, or R.B.N. However, the Russian government denied the allegations, stating that it was possible that individuals in Russia or elsewhere had taken it upon themselves to start the attacks.[318]

During the 2009 Iranian election protests, foreign activists seeking to help the opposition engaged in DDOS attacks against Iran's government. The official website of the Iranian government (ahmedinejad.ir) was rendered inaccessible on several occasions.[319]

Analysis by researchers indicates that the United States is highly vulnerable to cyber attack[320] and that China has been working hard to develop cyber warfare capabilities for approximately 20 years. In the event of a major conflict with the United States with a cyber dimension, an attacker might concentrate some of its most devastating attacks on American

---

[316] CERT Coordination Center, Software Engineering Institute, *Denial of Service Attacks* (Pittsburgh, PA: Carnegie Mellon University . *http://www.cert.org/tech_tips/denial_of_service.html.*

[317] Wikipedia, "Distributed Denial of Service Attacks on Root Nameservers." *http://en.wikipedia.org/wiki/Distributed_denial_of_service_attacks_on_root_nameservers.* The reference does not identify who runs the root servers that were attacked. Further research shows that in the February 2007 attack, at least six root servers were attacked but only two of them were noticeably affected: the "g-root," which is run by the U.S. Department of Defense and is physically based in Ohio, and the "I-root," run by the Internet Corporation for Assigned Names and Numbers (ICANN), which is physically based in California. Reference: *http://www.icann.org/en/announcements/factsheet-dns-attack-08mar07.pdf.*
October 2002 - The 13 domain name service root servers are designated "A" through "M." The most affected servers, according to Matrix NetSystems, were the "A" and "J" servers owned by VeriSign Global Registry Services in Herndon, Va.; the "G" server owned by the U.S. Department of Defense Network Information Center in Vienna, Va.; the "H" server at the U.S. Army Research Lab in Aberdeen, Md.; the "I" server, located in Stockholm; the "K" server, located in London; and the "M" server, located in Tokyo. This reference identifies seven of the nine servers: *http://news.cnet.com/Assault-on-Net-servers-fails/2100-1002_3-963005.html?tag=mncol.*

[318] John Markoff, "Before the Gunfire, Cyberattacks," *New York Times*, August 12, 2008. *http://www.nytimes.com/2008/08/13/technology/13cyber.html?ref=world.*

[319] Noah Shachtman, "Activists Launch Hack Attacks on Tehran Regime," *Wired*, June 15, 2009.

[320] Alex Spillius, "Cyber Attack 'Could Fell US Within 15 Minutes'," *Telegraph* (UK), May 7, 2010. *http://www.telegraph.co.uk/news/worldnews/northamerica/usa/7691500/Cyber-attack-could-fell-US-within-15-minutes.html.*

energy interests within the United States and abroad.[321] However, proving that a nation, such as China, is the source of such an attack would be very difficult, if even possible, due to the extremely fluid and dynamic nature of cyberspace.

A key fear among analysts is that the potential impact of cyber attacks remains poorly understood and potentially underestimated.[322] There are issues with how cyber attacks are classified and dealt with by decision makers: For example, cyber espionage is a form of attack but does not require the same type of response as a cyber intrusion that is perpetrated in order to create a cascading failure of a nation's power infrastructure or a malware attack intended to destroy data.

Comprehensive analysis has been done on China's cyber warfare capabilities, with conclusions indicating a mature capability with comprehensive doctrine and global reach:

> In a conflict with the US, China will likely use its CNO [computer network operation] capabilities to attack select nodes on the military's Non-classified Internet Protocol Router Network (NIPRNET) and unclassified DoD and civilian contractor logistics networks in the continental US (CONUS) and allied countries in the Asia-Pacific region. The stated goal in targeting these systems is to delay US deployments and impact combat effectiveness of troops already in theater. No authoritative PLA open source document identifies the specific criteria for employing [a] computer network attack against an adversary or what types of CNO actions PRC leaders believe constitutes an act of war. Ultimately, the only distinction between computer network exploitation and attack is the intent of the operator at the keyboard: The skill sets needed to penetrate a network for intelligence gathering purposes in peacetime are the same skills necessary to penetrate that network for offensive action during wartime. The difference is what the operator at that keyboard does with (or to) the information once inside the targeted network. If Chinese operators are, indeed, responsible for even some of the current exploitation efforts targeting US Government and commercial networks, then they may have already demonstrated that they possess a mature and operationally proficient CNO capability. [323]
>
> -- Northrop Grumman Corporation

---

[321] Daniel Ventre, "China's Strategy for Information Warfare: A Focus on Energy," *Journal of Energy Security* (May 18, 2010). *http://www.ensec.org/index.php?option=com_content&view=article&id=241:critical-energy-infrastructure-security-and-chinese-cyber-threats&catid=106:energysecuritycontent0510&Itemid=361*.

[322] Stephen M. Walt, "Is the cyber threat overblown?" *Foreign Policy* (March 30, 2010). *http://walt.foreignpolicy.com/posts/2010/03/30/is_the_cyber_threat_overblown?obref=obnetwork.*

[323] Northrop Grumman Corporation, *Capability of the People's Republic of China to Conduct Cyber Warfare and Computer Network Exploitation* (study performed on behalf of the U.S.-China Economic and Security Review Commission), October 16, 2009. *http://www.uscc.gov/researchpapers/2009/NorthropGrumman_PRC_Cyber_Paper_FINAL_Approved%20Report_16_Oct2009.pdf*.

GLOSSARY

1G	Analog cellular wireless -- in essence, the first generation of cellular wireless standards introduced in 1981.
2G	Digital cellular wireless, the second generation of cellular wireless standards introduced in 1992.
3G	The third generation of cellular wireless standards, introduced in 2002, based on International Mobile Telecommunications-2000, or "IMT-2000," also known as 3G or 3rd generation. In essence, 3G provides multimedia support, spread spectrum transmission, and at least 200 kbit/s broadband bandwidth. 3G is based on a family of standards for mobile telecommunications meeting specifications established by the International Telecommunication Union (ITU). 3G includes UMTS, CDMA2000, DECT (Digital Enhanced Cordless Telecommunications – a digital communication standard principally used for creating cordless phone systems), and WiMAX (Worldwide Interoperability for Microwave Access).
4G	The fourth generation of cellular wireless standards and a successor to the 1G, 2G, and 3G families of standards. In essence, 4G refers to all-IP-packet-switched networks, mobile ultrabroadband access (gigabit speed), and multicarrier transmission. Pre-4G technologies such as mobile WiMAX (available since 2006 – the proposed 802.16m standard) and 3G Long-Term Evolution (available since 2009 – LTE is considered a "3.9G" standard).
ANDROID	Google's operating system for mobile devices.
ASIC	Application-Specific Integrated Circuit.
BACKBONE	Primary transit networks or series of networks designed to carry data between different WANS or LANS. Backbones usually have greater data carrying capacity, or "bandwidth," than the networks they are interconnecting. The Internet Backbone is the interconnection of high-speed networks, primarily government, commercial telecommunications, and academic, that route data for Internet users.
BACKDOOR	A method of gaining remote control of a victim's computer through the use of a surreptitious means of entry built into a legitimate software or system. In essence, backdoors are created by configuring installed legitimate software to allow backdoor access, or through the installation of a specialized program designed to allow access under attacker-defined conditions. Trojan horse programs and rootkits often contain backdoor components.
BASIS-OF-TRADE	Relative trade or import/export strengths and weaknesses a nation or other entity has in relation to others and the marketplace in general.
BBP	A phone's Baseband Processor – the processor chipset that is designed to process signals for the telephone handset or system.
BLUETOOTH	Bluetooth is an open wireless technology standard for creating personal area networks (PANs) with high levels of security, and exchanging data over short distances using short-length radio waves from fixed and mobile devices. Bluetooth uses frequency-hopping spread spectrum, which breaks apart data being sent and transmits portions of it on up to 79 bands of 1 MHz width in the range 2402-2480 MHz, which is in the globally unlicensed Industrial, Scientific, and Medical (ISM) 2.4 GHz short-range radio frequency band.
BRIC	BRIC nations (Brazil, Russia, India, and China) in market analysis. An acronym used by Jim O'Neill during his time as head of global economic research at Goldman Sachs in 2001. According to a Goldman Sachs paper in 2005, Mexico and South Korea are comparable to the BRICs but were

excluded initially because their economies were considered to be more developed already. Goldman Sachs argued that due to rapid development in the BRIC, by 2050 their combined economies might eclipse the combined economies of the current richest nations. Combined, the BRIC accounts for more than 25 percent of the world's land area and more than 40 percent of global population.

BROADBAND	An Internet connection with a much larger capacity than dial-up or ISDN (typically greater than 200 kilobits/per second).
CDMA2000	A family of 3G mobile technology standards that use CDMA channel access to send voice, data, and signaling data between mobile phones and cell sites.
CFIUS	Committee on Foreign Investment in the United States – an interagency committee of the U.S. government that reviews national security implications of foreign investments in U.S. companies or markets. *http://www.treas.gov/offices/international-affairs/cfius*
CHIPSETS	A set of specialized chips in a system's main, peripheral, or expansion circuitry.
CIC	China Investment Corporation, headquartered in Beijing. *http://www.china-inv.cn/cicen.*
CNA	Computer Network Attack – The use of computer networks to disrupt, deny, degrade, or destroy information resident in computers and computer networks or the computers and networks themselves.
CNCI	Comprehensive National Cybersecurity Initiative. *http://www.whitehouse.gov/cybersecurity/comprehensive-national-cybersecurity-initiative.*
CND	Computer Network Defense – The use of computer networks to protect, monitor, analyze, detect, and respond to unauthorized activity within information systems and computer networks.
CNE	Computer Network Exploitation – Enabling operations and intelligence collection through computer networks to gather data from target systems or networks.
CNO	Computer Network Operations – encompasses Computer Network Attack (CNA), Computer Network Defense (CND), and Computer Network Exploitation (CNE).
CONUS	Continental United States. Typically refers to being geographically located within the boundaries of the 48 contiguous states of the United States. CONUS does not typically include Hawaii and Alaska or the outlying territories (Guam, Puerto Rico, etc.).
CPU	Central Processing Unit – the central processor portion of a computer system that carries out the main instructions of a computer program and is the primary element carrying out the computer's functions.
CYBER SECURITY	Security against electronic attacks, such as cyber warfare and other forms of hostile CNO.
DATACOM	Data Communications.
DDOS	Distributed Denial of Service (DDOS) attacks – attacks that consume computing or communications resources by engaging many intermediate (or proxy) computers simultaneously to attack one or a few victims with a flood of traffic and system requests. The purpose is to flood target systems with so much traffic and/or so many computational requests that no other traffic can get through or no other useful functions can occur. Intermediate or proxy systems used in DDOS attacks have often been previously compromised and are under the control of hostile actors.
DNS	Domain Name Server.
DRAM	Dynamic random access memory – a type of random access memory that stores each bit of data in a separate capacitor within an integrated circuit.
DSL	A family of technologies that provides digital data transmission over the wires

of a local telephone network. This is typically a terrestrially based technology for providing broadband services over legacy copper-wire infrastructures of PSTNs (Public Switched Telecommunications Network).

DSP
Digital signal processing--a specialized microprocessor with an architecture optimized for digital signal processing.

EDGE
Enhanced Data rates for GSM Evolution (EDGE) – also known as Enhanced GPRS (EGPRS), IMT Single Carrier (IMT-SC), or "Enhanced Data rates for Global Evolution." A backward-compatible digital mobile phone technology allowing improved data transmission rates on top of standard GSM.

ELECTRO-OPTICAL
Pertaining to effects of an electric field on the optical properties of a material.

ESSENTIAL PATENTS
Patents that disclose and claim one or more inventions that are required to practice a given industry standard. Standardization bodies often require that members disclose and grant licenses to patents and pending patent applications that they own and that cover a standard that the body is developing. If standards bodies fail to get licenses to all patents that are essential to practicing a standard, then the owners of those unlicensed patents can often demand royalties from those who ultimately adopt the standards.

ETHERNET
A set of network cabling and network access (CSMA/CD) protocol standards for bus topology computer networks invented by Xerox Corporation and now managed by the 802.3 subcommittee of the IEEE (Institute of Electrical and Electronics Engineers).

EV-DO
"Evolution-Data Optimized" or "Evolution-Data Only," abbreviated as EV-DO or EVDO and often EV, is a 3G telecommunications standard for the wireless transmission of data through radio signals for broadband Internet access.

FAR
The U.S. government's Federal Acquisition Regulation – the principal set of rules in the Federal Acquisition Regulation System.

FIB
Focused-Ion-Beam.

FIREWALL
Part of a system or network designed to block unauthorized access while permitting authorized communications.

FREQUENCY DIVISION
Frequency-Division Duplexing (FDD) means that the transmitter and receiver operate at different carrier frequencies.

FREQUENCY-HOPPING SPREAD-SPECTRUM
A method of transmitting radio signals by rapidly switching a carrier among many frequency channels using pseudo-random sequences known to transmitter and receiver pairs or groups.

FTP
File Transfer Protocol - A standard Internet protocol implemented in FTP server and client software and most web browsers to "transfer data reliably and efficiently."

GPS
The U.S. Global Positioning System.

GSE
Government-sponsored enterprises--a group of financial services corporations created by the United States Congress. GSEs' function is to enhance the flow of credit to targeted sectors of the economy and to make those segments of the capital market more efficient and transparent. Residential mortgage borrowing is the largest of the borrowing segments in which the GSEs operate, in which they hold approximately $5 trillion worth of mortgages.

GSM
Global System for Mobile Communications – a wireless mobile telephone standard in use broadly on a worldwide basis.

HACKER
An individual using computer technology in hostile or nefarious ways generally not originally intended by the publisher or manufacturer. In essence, people who attack others using computers or networks.

HOTSPOT
A physical site that offers Internet access over a wireless local area network.

HSDPA	Hotspots are typically based on WiFi technology. High-Speed Downlink Packet Access.
HTTP	Hypertext Transfer Protocol – The message format and exchange standard used by web browsers and web servers.
HUB	An unintelligent device for connecting multiple twisted pair or fiber-optic Ethernet devices together and making them act as a single network segment. Hubs work at the physical layer (layer 1) of the OSI model. Hubs are a form of multiport repeater.
IC	Integrated Circuit.
IDS	Intrusion Detection System – A computer or network monitoring system capable of matching observed phenomenon to patterns of known or suspected unauthorized activity and using this as a basis for intercepting penetrations by hostile users or applications.
IEEE	Institute of Electrical and Electronics Engineers.
INFOCON	Information Operations Condition – INFOCON classifications mirror those used in the Defense Conditions (DEFCON) Alert System and are a uniform system of five progressive readiness conditions (INFOCON 5 thru INFOCON 1). INFOCON 5 indicates nominal conditions at normal levels of readiness. INFOCON-1 indicates a maximum level of high alert due to impending severe threat or attack. As INFOCON levels increase, elements of network functionality or services deemed lower priority or at high risk of attack may be temporarily suspended. Offensive CNA tools used by hostile attackers that might be effective during an INFOCON-5 normal state of readiness may be rendered ineffective if the services or applications they exploit are turned off.
INTERNET	Global networks of computers that communicate using Internet Protocol (IP) and Border Gateway Protocol (BGP) to identify the best paths to route communications between end-points.
IP ADDRESS	Internet Protocol Address – a number assigned to each computer's or other device's network interface(s) that are active on a network supporting the Internet Protocol.
IP TELEPHONY	Voice over Internet Protocol (VoIP) is a general term for a family of transmission technologies that deliver voice communications over IP networks (the Internet or other packet-switched networks). Other terms frequently encountered and synonymous with VoIP are "IP Telephony," "Internet Telephony," Voice Over Broadband (VoBB), "Broadband Telephony," and "Broadband Phone." Communications services (voice, facsimile, and/or voice-messaging applications) that are transported via the Internet rather than the public switched telephone network (PSTN).
IPS	Intrusion Prevention System – an inline system or software that applies IDS-style logic and approves or rejects network traffic, program and data access, hardware use, etc. Where an IDS is designed to detect intrusions that are in progress and intercept/manage them before they progress too far, an IPS is designed to prevent intrusions from gaining any penetration whatsoever.
IPV4	Internet Protocol version 4 is the fourth revision in the development of the Internet Protocol and the first version of the protocol to be widely deployed. A connectionless protocol for use on packet-switched Link Layer networks such as Ethernet. IPv4 operates on a "best effort" delivery model that does not guarantee delivery, proper sequencing, or duplicate delivery. Delivery and data integrity are addressed by TCP (Transmission Control Protocol), an upper-layer transmission control protocol – hence the common acronym "TCP/IP". IPv4 uses 32-bit (four-byte) addresses, limiting address space to 4,294,967,296 possible unique addresses. Some are reserved for special purposes, such as private networks (~18 million addresses) or multicast addresses (~270 million addresses), reducing the number of addresses that potentially can be allocated for routing on the public Internet. IPv4 address

	shortages have been developing and will eventually result in exhaustion of IPv4 address space, which has led to development of the IPv6 protocol as a long-term solution.
IPV6	Internet Protocol version 6 is an Internet Protocol version that is designed to succeed IPv4. IPv6 was defined in December 1998 by the IETF (Internet Engineering Task Force) with publication of RFC 2460. IPv6 has a larger address space than IPv4 due to the use of a 128-bit address versus IPv4's 32-bit address. IPv6's new address space supports 2^{128} (about 3.4×10^{38}) addresses. This dramatic expansion provides flexibility in allocating addresses and routing traffic and eliminates the widespread need for network address translation (NAT). IPv6 is a vastly improved protocol standard that incorporates many new enhancements over IPv4 in addition to a vastly increased address space. New routing techniques, expanded protocol capabilities, enhanced security, and other improvements are available in IPv6.
ISP	Internet Service Provider.
IW	Information Warfare – Efforts to achieve information superiority by affecting adversary information, information-based processes, information systems, and computer-based networks while defending one's own resources.
IXP	Internet Exchange Point (IX or IXP) – a physical infrastructure through which Internet service providers exchange Internet traffic between their networks.
JAILBREAKING	A process that allows iPad, iPhone, and iPod Touch users to run any software code on their devices, as opposed to only code authorized by Apple. Once jailbroken, device users are able to download many extensions and themes previously unavailable through Apple's App Store, via pirated or unofficial means.
LAN	Local Area Network – an interconnection of computers that are in relatively close proximity to one another, such as within a building.
LAST-MILE	The "last mile" or "last kilometer" is the final leg of delivering connectivity from a communications provider to a customer.
LEGACY	Systems or applications that continue to be used beyond intended service life because users do not want to replace or redesign them.
LMR	Land Mobile Radio – a wireless communications system intended for use by terrestrial users in vehicles (mobile) or on foot (portable). LMR is typically used by emergency first responder, public works, or companies with large numbers of vehicle or field staff. LMR systems may be independent but often are connected to other fixed systems such as the public switched telephone network (PSTN) or cellular networks.
LTE	Long-Term Evolution), also known as "3.9G," is the trademarked project name of a high-performance air interface for cellular mobile telephony. It is a project of the 3rd Generation Partnership Project (3GPP), operating under a name trademarked by the European Telecommunications Standards Institute. The current generation of mobile telecommunication networks are collectively known as 3G (for "third generation"). Although LTE is often marketed as 4G, LTE is actually a 3.9G technology (pre-4G). LTE does not fully comply with IMT Advanced 4G requirements. As a pre-4G standard, LTE is evolving into "LTE Advanced," a 4th generation standard (4G) radio technology.
MACRO LEVEL	Characterizes societies or systems as a whole, rather than parts (meso- or microlevels).
MICROCHIP	An integrated circuit (also known as IC, microcircuit, microchip, silicon chip, or chip). Miniaturized electronic circuits that consist mainly of semiconductor devices and other passive components and that are manufactured in the surface of thin substrates of semiconductor materials.
MIIT	The Ministry of Industry and Information Technology of the People's Republic of China. *http://www.miit.gov.cn.*
MOTHERBOARD	The main or central circuit board in modern computers that holds many crucial system components and provides connectors for other accessory system

	components and peripherals.
MPU	Microprocessor Unit – a term occasionally used to describe a CPU (Central Processor Unit).
NBA	Network Behavioral Analysis – intrusion detection systems that detect and model network traffic to discern and analyze violations of known benign activities.
NIPRNET	Nonclassified Internet Protocol Router Network. A network of the U.S. Department of Defense providing unclassified Internet access and interconnectivity to DOD users and facilities.
NODE	Typically, the individual devices or computers on a network.
OBEX	OBEX (OBject EXchange), and IrOBEX (Infrared OBEX), is a communications protocol facilitating exchange of binary data between devices. The OBEX standard is managed by the Infrared Data Association and has also been adopted by the Bluetooth Special Interest Group and the SyncML wing of the Open Mobile Alliance (OMA).
OCONUS	Outside of the geographic boundary of the contiguous 48 states of the United States. In essence, the opposite of CONUS.
OUTSOURCING	Transfer of a potentially internal business function to an external service provider.
PBX	Private Branch Exchange – a telecommunications switching system, usually physically located at a customer's place of business, providing internal communication between users and access to outside (trunk) telephone lines.
PHOTODETECTOR	Any device used to detect electromagnetic radiation.
PROGRAMMABLE LOGIC ARRAY	Programmable devices used to implement combinational logic circuits.
RENMINBI (RMB)	The renminbi is the official physical currency of the People's Republic of China, whose principal unit of account is the yuan ("¥" or "CNY"). The currency is legal tender in mainland China but not in Hong Kong and Macau. Renminbi translates as people's currency. The renminbi is issued by the People's Bank of China, the monetary authority of the PRC. In practice, use of "renminbi" is analogous to the use of "sterling" within the United Kingdom, where sterling is the actual physical currency but the Pound is the official unit of account by which sterling are denominated.
REPEATER	An electronic device that receives a signal and retransmits it at a higher level and/or higher power, or onto the other side of an obstruction, so that the signal can cover longer distances.
RFC	Request for Comments, an IETF (Internet Engineering Task Force) memorandum on Internet systems and standards.
ROOTKIT	Software used by a second or third party after gaining access to a computer system in order to conceal alteration of files, file systems, or processes without the user's knowledge.
ROUTER	Telecommunications devices that direct packets of information using OSI layer 3 (network layer) information. Also describes Internet devices that connect local area networks to form larger Internets.
SAFE	The State Administration of Foreign Exchange (SAFE), a Chinese government body that manages China's foreign exchange reserves. http://www.safe.gov.cn.
SERVICE FOOTPRINT	An area of services coverage. Typically, the geographic area within which a service may be provided.
SMART PHONES	Mobile phones that offer more advanced computing abilities and connectivity than basic "feature phones." Some feature phones are able to run simple applications based on generic platforms such as Java; smart phones allow much more advanced applications. Smart phones run complete operating systems and provide platforms for application developers. They may be considered handheld computers with mobile telephone capabilities.

SMS	Short Message Service is the text communication service component of mobile communication systems. Standard communications protocols allow the exchange of SMS messages between mobile phone devices.
SPYWARE	Malware intended to be installed on a user's system to surreptitiously collect incremental information about users.
SRAM	Static Random Access Memory – semiconductor memory where, unlike dynamic RAM (DRAM), it does not need to be periodically refreshed. SRAM uses bistable latching circuitry to store each bit.
STRUCTURED ASIC	Structured ASIC design (also "Platform ASIC") has a variety of contextual meanings. The basic premise infers that both manufacturing cycle time and design cycle time are reduced compared to cell-based ASIC. Predefined metal layers reduce manufacturing time, and precharacterization of what is on the silicon reduces design cycle time.
SUPPLY CHAIN	Systems of organizations, people, technology, activities, information, and resources involved in moving products or services from suppliers to customers/users.
SWITCHES	Network switches are computer networking devices that connect network segments. The term commonly refers to network bridges that process and route data at data link layers (layer 2) of the OSI model. Switches that additionally process data at the network layer (layer 3 and above) are often referred to as Layer 3 switches or multilayer switches. The term network switch does not generally encompass unintelligent or passive network devices such as hubs and repeaters.
TIME DIVISION	Digital or analog multiplexing in which two or more signals or bit-streams are transferred simultaneously as subchannels in one communication channel while physically taking turns on the channel.
TROJAN	Non-self-replicating malware that appears to perform desirable functions for users but instead facilitates unauthorized access to user computer systems.
USB	Universal Serial Bus – a "serial bus" standard for connecting devices.
UV	Ultraviolet.
WAN	Wide Area Network – computer networks covering large geographic areas and that can refer to several buildings in a city or several cities. A WAN can also refer to a group of LANs connected by dedicated long-distance links.
WCDMA	Wideband Code Division Multiple Access, UMTS-FDD, UTRA-FDD, or IMT-2000 CDMA Direct Spread – a wireless interface standard in 3G mobile telecommunications networks.
WiFi	A wireless local area network model based on the IEEE 802.11 standards and the most widely used WLAN technology today.
WiMAX	Worldwide Interoperability for Microwave Access – a telecommunications technology providing wireless data, voice, and video over long distances. Currently provides fixed and fully mobile Internet access up to 40 Mbit/s based on the IEEE 802.16 standard and is expected to offer up to 1 Gbit/s fixed speeds with the IEEE 802.16m update.
WIRELESS CHARGING	Inductive Charging – a technology using the electromagnetic fields to transfer energy between objects.
WORM	Self-replicating malware computer programs that use computer networks to (potentially) automatically, autonomously, and/or surreptitiously send copies of themselves to other nodes/systems.
YUÁN	A cause of some confusion, a "yuan" ("元" or "CNY") is the base unit of a number of modern Chinese currencies. Distinction between the yuan and a renminbi (a name also used for the Chinese currency) can be viewed as analogous to that between the pound and sterling in Great Britain. The yuan is the unit of account, and a renminbi is the actual physical scrip or change of currency. The symbol for the yuan "元" may also be used in some circumstances to refer to the currency units of Japan and Korea and also to

ZERO-DAY

translate the currency unit of a dollar relative to yuan. The U.S. dollar is called Měiyuán or American yuan, in Chinese. When used in English in the context of the modern foreign exchange market, the Chinese yuan most commonly refers to the renminbi but may be indicated by the simple symbol of a yuan (CNY).

Zero-day (or zero-hour or day-zero) attacks or threats are attempts to exploit system or application vulnerabilities that are currently (at the time of attack) unknown or undisclosed to software developers and users.

APPENDIX C
PARTIAL BIBLIOGRAPHY

- "Asia Private Equity Review," April 2006. Reprinted in China C SR.com, May 27, 2008.
- Adee, Sally. "The Hunt for the Kill Switch." *IEEE Spectrum*, May 2008. *http://www. spectrum.ieee.org/semiconductors/design/the-hunt-for-the-kill-switch*.
- Agence France-Presse, "China cements role as top creditor to US: Treasury," March 17, 2009. *http://www.google.com/hostednews/afp/article/ALeqM5hqDfBfaypzFV7bvJ1j3vkN0qW8A g*.
- Alcatel Alenia Press Release. "Alcatel Alenia Space Wins New Communication and Broadcast Satellite Contract Chinasat 6B From ChinaSatcom, Bolstering Cooperation With China." Available at Red Orbit.com. December 5, 2005,. *http://www.redorbit.com/news/space/1838943/esa_and_thales_alenia_space_enter_neg otiations_for_mtg/index.html*.
- AllBusiness.Com. "Qualcomm, China TechFaith Create Wireless Company." March 27, 2009.
- *Asia Times*, "China's trillion-dollar kitty is ready," October 2, 2007. *http://www.atimes.com/atimes/China_Business/IJ02Cb01.html*.
- *Asia Times,* "3G is Key to a Foreign Telecom Role in China," December 6', 2006. *http://www.atimes.com/atimes/China_Business/HL06Cb02.html*.
- Bhagat, Sanjai. Reforming Executive Compensation: Focusing and Committing to the Long-term. New Haven, CT: Yale Law School, February 2009. *http://www.law.yale.edu/documents/pdf/cbl/Bhagat_Romano_Reforming_Executive.pdf.*
- Blakely, Rhys, et al. "MI5 Alert on China's Cyberspace Spy Threat." *Times (London)*, December 1, 2007. *http://business.timesonline.co.uk/tol/business/industry_sectors/technology/article298025 0.ece*.
- Bliss, Jeff. "China's Spying Overwhelms U.S. Counterintelligence." Bloomberg.com. April 2, 2007. *http://www.bloomberg.com/apps/news?pid=20601087&sid=ab2PiDl1qW9Q&refer=home*.
- *Bloomberg Businessweek*. Huawei Confirms Plans for Handset Division Sale. June 10, 2008. *http://www.businessweek.com/globalbiz/content/jun2008/gb20080619_118434.htm?cam paign_id=rss_as*.
- Bounds, Jeff. "Huawei to Add Hundreds of Tech Jobs." *Texas Business Journal* (May 1, 2009). *http://dallas.bizjournals.com/dallas/stories/2009/05/04/story15.html*.
- Brown, Paul B. "Trojan Horse on a Chip." *New York Times*, April 5, 2008. *http://www.nytimes.com/2008/04/05/business/05offline.html.*
- C114.net. "Alcatel Lucent chases profits, three years on." January 6, 2010. *http://www.cn-c114.net/583/a473644.html*.
- *Caijing China,* "The 3Com Deal, Behind the Security Flap," October 23, 2007. *http://www.cn-c114.net/582/a314041.html*.
- Carew, Rick. "China Seeks External Help for Wealth Fund." *Wall Street Journal*, December 14, 2007. *http://online.wsj.com/article/SB119759666432928557.html*.
- Carew, Rick. "Great Wall Street of China." *Wall Street Journal*, December 20, 2007. *http://online.wsj.com/article/SB119805649734239175.html*.

- Carnegie Endowment for International Peace. "China Mainland." Commentary and Analysis. 2010. *http://www.carnegieendowment.org/regions/?fa=viewRegions&region=1000185*.
- Carnegie Endowment for International Peace. "Chinese Economy." Commentary and Analysis. 2010. *http://www.carnegieendowment.org/topic/?fa=viewTopic&topic=3000164*.
- Carnegie Mellon University. "Denial of Service Attacks." Pittsburgh, PA: CERT Coordination Center, Software Engineering Institute, June 4, 2001 (updated). *http://www.cert.org/tech_tips/denial_of_service.html*.
- *Cellular-News*. "Huawei Taps Former Nortel Exec to European Job," July 13, 2009. *http://www.cellular-news.com/story/38491.php*.
- Chang, Maria Hsia. "China Policy of Engagement Needs an Overhaul." *San Francisco Chronicle*, June 7, 1999, p. A23. *http://articles.sfgate.com/1999-06-07/opinion/17692104_1_senkaku-china-last-summer-diaoyu*.
- Cheng, Dean. "PLA Views on Space: The Prerequisite for Information Dominance." Alexandria, VA: Center for Naval Analysis, October 2007. *http://www.cna.org/documents/5.pdf*.
- *China Daily*, "China's telecoms sector gets 3G licenses," January 7, 2009. *http://www.chinadaily.com.cn/bizchina/2009-01/07/content_7375721.htm*.
- *China Daily*, "China Finally Awards Telecom Operators 3G Wireless," January 7, 2009. *http://www.chinadaily.com.cn/bizchina/2009-01/07/content_7374321.htm*.
- *China Daily*, "Huawei Puts Terminal Unit Sale on Hold," October 10, 2008. *http://www.chinadaily.com.cn/business/2008-10/10/content_7094113.htm*.
- ChinaTechNews.com. "Indian Government Bans Import of Chinese Telecom Equipment." April 30, 2010. *http://www.chinatechnews.com/2010/04/30/11981-indian-government-bans-import-of-chinese-telecom-equipment*.
- ChinaTechNews.com. "Pakistan Welcomes More Chinese Telecom Investment." February 18, 2009. *http://www.chinatechnews.com/2009/02/18/8855-pakistan-welcomes-more-chinese-telecom-investment*.
- Christensen, Thomas J. "Windows and War: Trend Analysis and Beijing's Use of Force." In *New Directions in the Study of China's Foreign Policy*. Edited by Alastair Iain Johnston and Robert Ross. Palo Alto, CA: Stanford University Press, 2006. *http://www.sup.org/book.cgi?id=9777*.
- Coleman, Kevin. "Private Sector-Military Collaboration Vital To Confront Cyber Threats." Defense Tech. April 19, 2010. *http://defensetech.org/2010/04/19/private-sector-military-collaboration-vital-to-confront-cyber-threats/#ixzz0oBCGbUKY*.
- Collingridge, David. *The Social Control of Technology*. New York, NY: St. Martin's Press, 1980.
- Cowen Latitude. *Technology and Telecom Sector M&A Report 1st Quarter 2009*. *http://www.cowenlatitude.com/document/09q1_china_tech_ma.pdf*.
- CSC Staff. "Krugman in China: Stimulating, Controversial, and Expensive." *ChinaStakes* (Shanghai), May 16, 2009. ChinaStakes.com *http://www.chinastakes.com/2009/5/krugman-in-china-stimulating-controversial-and-expensive.html*.
- Dalrymple, Jim. "Apple Fixes iPhone SMS Flaw." CNet.com. July 31, 2009, *http://news.cnet.com/8301-1009_3-10301001-83.html*.
- Dambala, Inc. "The Command Structure of the Aurora Botnet, History, Patterns and Findings." March 3, 2010. *http://www.damballa.com/downloads/r_pubs/Aurora_Botnet_Command_Structure.pdf*.

- Del Oro Group Press Release. "Chinese Vendors Huawei and ZTE Gain Ground on Leaders Ericsson and Nokia Siemens." April 26, 2010. *http://www.delloro.com/news/2010/WPC042610.htm*.
- Derene, Glenn, and Joan Pappalardo. "Counterfeit Chips Raise Big Hacking, Terror Threats, Experts Say." *Popular Mechanics*, October 1, 2009. *http://www.popularmechanics.com/technology/gadgets/news/4253628*.
- DeWeese, Steve, et al. *Capability of the People's Republic of China to Conduct Cyber Warfare and Computer Network Exploitation.* Northrop Grumman Corporation for the U.S.-China Economic and Security Review Commission, October 16, 2009. *http://www.uscc.gov/researchpapers/2009/NorthropGrumman_PRC_Cyber_Paper_FINAL_Approved%20Report_16Oct2009.pdf*.
- Dezan Shira & Associates.*Made in USA: China and India Invest Abroad.* May 13, 2010. *http://www.2point6billion.com/news/2010/05/13/made-in-usa-china-and-india-invest-abroad-5645.html*.
- Edgerton, David. *The Shock of the Old: Technology and Global History Since 1900.* New York: Oxford University Press, 2006. *http://www.oup.com/us/catalog/general/subject/HistoryOther/HistoryofTechnology/?view=usa&ci=9780195322835*.
- Einhorn, Bruce. Huawei's 3Com Deal Flops. *Business Week*, February 21, 2008. *http://www.businessweek.com/globalbiz/blog/eyeonasia/archives/2008/02/huaweis_3com_deal_flops.html*.
- Elgan, Mike. "Is China Cyber-Stealing Your Secrets?" *Datamation*, September 17, 2009. *http://itmanagement.earthweb.com/secu/article.php/3839541/Is-China-Cyber-Stealing-Your-Secrets.htm*.
- Enck, William, et al. *Exploiting Open Functionality in SMS-Capable Cellular Networks.* University Park, PA: Pennsylvania State University, September 2, 2005. *http://www.smsanalysis.org/smsanalysis.pdf*.
- Engels, Daniel W., et al. "Improving Visibility in the DOD Supply Chain." June 2004. *http://www.almc.army.mil/alog/issues/mayJun04/alog_supple%20chain.htm*.
- Engineering Trends.com. "What is Happening To Computer Science and Engineering?" Report 1005E, October 2005. *http://www.engtrends.com/IEE/1005E.php*.
- Fallows, James. The $1.4 Trillion Question, The Chinese are subsidizing the American way of life. Are we playing them for suckers—or are they playing us? *Atlantic* (January/February 2008). *http://www.theatlantic.com/doc/200801/fallows-chinese-dollars/4*.
- Fallows. James. The $1.4 Trillion Dollar Question. *Atlantic Monthly*, January/February 2008. *http://www.theatlantic.com/doc/200801/fallows-chinese-dollars*.
- *Federal Communications Law Journal.* June 6, 2005.
- Fierce Wireless; Huawei Website. "Huawei to deploy CDMA 2000 infrastructure for Cricket Communications." July 11, 2007. *http://www.huawei.com/news/view.do?id=4445&cid=42*.
- Fisher, Richard Jr. *People's Liberation Army Leverage of Foreign Military Technology.* Alexandria, VA: International Assessment and Strategy Center, March 22, 2006. *http://www.strategycenter.net/research/pubID.97/pub_detail.asp*.
- *Forbes.* Huawei Buys Back Into 3Com. October 1, 2007. *http://www.forbes.com/2009/03/27/huawei-security-clearwire-technology-enterprise-tech-huawei.html*.
- Fox News. "Experts: Zombie Cell-Phone Hack Attacks May Be Next." October 16, 2008. *http://www.foxnews.com/story/0,2933,438481,00.html*.
- Gasper, Peter D. "Cyber Threat to Critical Infrastructure - 2010-2015." Paper presented at the Idaho National Laboratory," Information & Cyberspace Symposium, Fort

Leavenworth, KS., September 22-24, 2008.
http://usacac.army.mil/cac2/cew/repository/papers/Cyber_Threat_to_CI.PDF.

- Global Crossing Press Release. "Global Crossing to Acquire Global Marine Subsidiary of Cable and Wireless." April 26, 1999; and Funding Universe. Global Crossing backgrounder. 10Ks and Annual Report Data.
- Goetz, John, and Marcel Rosenbach. "Cyber Spies: 'GhostNet' and the New World of Espionage." *Der Speigel* online, April 10, 2009. *http://www.spiegel.de/international/world/0,1518,618478,00.html*.
- Goodall, Randy. "External Programs: Briefing to the Defense Science Board Task Force on High-performance Microchip Supply." June 23, 2004. *http://www.acq.osd.mil/dsb/reports/ADA435563.pdf*.
- Goodchild, Joan. "3 Simple Steps to Hack a Cell Phone."CSOonline.com. April 29, 2009. *http://www.csoonline.com/article/491200/_Simple_Steps_to_Hack_a_Smartphone_Inclu des_Video_*.
- Goodchild, Joan. "CISCO: SMS Smartphone Attacks on the Rise." CSOonline.com. July 14, 2009. *http://www.csoonline.com/article/497120/Cisco_SMS_Smartphone_Attacks_on_the_Ris e.*
- Gorman, S.P. *Networks, security and complexity: the role of public policy in critical infrastructure protection.* Cheltenham, England: Edward Elgar Publishing, 2005.
- Greenberg, Andy. "The Deal that Could Have Saved Nortel." *Forbes,* January 14, 2009. *http://www.forbes.com/2009/01/14/nortel-huawei-china-tech-wire- cx_ag_0114nortel.html*.
- Greenberg, Andy. Nortel's China Syndrome. *Forbes,* January 12, 2009. *http://www.forbes.com/2009/01/11/nortel-huawei-buyout-tech-enter- cx_ag_0112nortel.html*.
- Greenberg, Andy. "Nortel's China Syndrome, Concerns over Chinese cyber-spying may have stalled a deal with Huawei that Nortel needs." Forbes.com. January 12, 2009. *http://www.forbes.com/2009/01/11/nortel-huawei-buyout-tech-enter- cx_ag_0112nortel.html*.
- Greenberg, Andy. Huawei's U.S. coming out Party. *Forbes,* March 27, 2009. *http://www.forbes.com/2009/03/27/huawei-security-clearwire-technology-enterprise-tech- huawei.html.*
- Grow, Brian, et al. The New E-spionage Threat. *BusinessWeek,* April 10, 2008. http://www.businessweek.com/magazine/content/08_16/b4080032218430.htm.
- Harris, Shane. "China's Cyber-Militia." *National Journal,* May 31, 2008. *http://www.nationaljournal.com/njmagazine/cs_20080531_6948.php*.
- Hewlett Packard Press Release. "H.P. to Acquire 3Com for $2.7 billion." November 11, 2009. *http://www.hp.com/hpinfo/newsroom/press/2009/091111xa.html.*
- Hobsbawm, Eric. *The Age of Revolution: Europe 1789–1848.* London: Weidenfeld & Nicolson Ltd., 1996 (paperback).
- House Armed Services Committee. Subcommittee on Terrorism, Unconventional Threats, and Capabilities. *Information Technology.* Statement by Michael E. Krieger. 111th Cong., 2nd sess., May 5, 2009.
- House Committee on Homeland Security. Subcommittee on Emerging Threats, Cybersecurity, and Science and Technology. "Addressing the Nation's Cyber Security Challenges: Reducing Vulnerabilities Requires Strategic Investment and Immediate Action." Testimony of O. Sami Saydjari. 110th Cong., 1st sess., April 25, 2007. *http://homeland.house.gov/SiteDocuments/20070425145307-82503.pdf*.

http://nobelprize.org/educational/economics/trade/ohlin.html.

- Hutchison Whampoa Limited Press Release. "Hutchison Whampoa and Global Crossing complete telecom joint Venture in Hong Kong." January 12, 2000. *http://www.hutchison-whampoa.com/eng/media/press_releases/press_releases.htm?category=Corporate&fyear=&show=all*.

- *InformationWeek*. FCC Approves Sprint Clearwire Merger, National WiMAX Coming. November 5, 2008. *http://www.informationweek.com/news/telecom/business/showArticle.jhtml?articleID=212000757*.

- *InfoTech News*. Research and Markets: Gigabit Ethernet Fiber and Copper Cabling Systems.TMCNET.com. April 15, 2010. *http://it.tmcnet.com/news/2010/04/15/4731374.htm*.

- Jackson, David. "China Mobile - Millicom Deal Threatens Ericsson, Nokia, Lucent, Motorola, QualComm." Seekingalpha.com. May 25, 2006. *http://seekingalpha.com/article/11224-china-mobile-millicom-deal-threatens-ericsson-nokia-lucent-motorola-qualcom*.

- Jenkins, Holman W. Jr. "China, Google and the Cloud Wars, Your personal data still aren't safe." *Wall Street Journal*, January 22, 2010. *http://online.wsj.com/article/SB10001424052748703699204575016801501346056.html*.

- Jie, Liu. "Curbing overcapacity, stimulating consumption key for China's economic revival." Xinhua, January 7, 2010. Chinaview.cn, *http://news.xinhuanet.com/english/2010-01/07/content_12771682.htm*.

- Kanwal, Gurmeet. "China's Emerging Cyber War Doctrine."*Journal of Defence Studies* Vol. 3, No 3 (July 2009). *http://www.idsa.in/system/files/jds_3_3_gkanwal_0.pdf*.

- Kou, Kaiser. "China's 4G Master Plan." February 26, 2008. *http://digitalwatch.ogilvy.com.cn/en/?p=205*.

- Kravets, David. "iPhone Jailbreaking Could Crash Cellphone Towers, Apple Claims." *Wired*, July 28, 2009. *http://www.wired.com/threatlevel/2009/07/jailbreak/*.

- Kwok, Vivian Wai-yin. "China Investment Corp. Flashes its Yuan." Forbes.com, May 5, 2007. *http://www.forbes.com/2007/10/05/china-investment-fund-markets-equity-cx_vk_1005markets03.html.*

- Lewis, James A., et al. *Securing Cyberspace for the 44th Presidency*. Washington, DC: Center for Strategic and International Studies, CSIS Commission on Cybersecurity for the 44th Presidency, December 8, 2008. *http://csis.org/publication/securing-cyberspace-44th-presidency*.

- Light Reading Mobile. "Clearwire Confirms Huawei Deal." August 11, 2009. *http://www.lightreading.com/document.asp?doc_id=180326*.

- Light Reading; Cable Digital News. "Cox, Huawei Make Wireless Connection." March 30, 2009. *http://www.lightreading.com/document.asp?doc_id=174434&site=lr_cable*.

- LightReading. "Huawei Supplies Leap Wireless." August 15, 2006. *http://www.lightreading.com/document.asp?doc_id=101446*.

- Manji, Firoze, and Stephen Marks. "African Perspectives on China in Africa." Fahamu--Networks for Social Justice. 2007.

- Manye, Kevin. "The New Face of IBM" - "China's biggest IT brand wants to go global. So it bought the PC division - and the world-class management - of an American icon. Who says being "oceans apart" is a bad thing?" Wired.com, July 2005. *http://www.wired.com/wired/archive/13.07/lenovo.html*.

- MarketWatch Inc. "Taiwan stocks on fire on China Mobile-Far EasTone." April 29, 2009. *http://www.marketwatch.com/story/china-mobiles-taiwan-plan-could-change-everything*.

- Markoff, John, and David Barboza. "Academic Paper in China Sets Off Alarms in U.S." *New York Times*, March 20, 2010. *http://www.nytimes.com/2010/03/21/world/asia/21grid.html*.

- Markoff, John. "Before the Gunfire, Cyberattacks." *New York Times*, August 12, 2008. *http://www.nytimes.com/2008/08/13/technology/13cyber.html?ref=world*.
- Marquand, Robert, and Ben Arnoldy. "China Emerges as Leader in Cyberwarfare." *Christian Science Monitor*, September 14, 2007. *http://www.csmonitor.com/2007/0914/p01s01-woap.html*.
- Marsan, Carolyn Duffy. Invisible IPv6 Traffic Poses Serious Network Threat. *Network World*, July 13, 2009. *http://www.networkworld.com/news/2009/071309-rogue-ipv6.html*.
- Martin, Michael F. China's Sovereign Wealth Fund. *Sovereign Wealth Fund News*, January 22, 2008. *http://www.sovereignwealthfundsnews.com/safe.php*. Also, Congressional Reporting Service. *http://www.fas.org/sgp/crs/row/RL34337.pdf*.
- *Mass High Tech*: *The Journal* of *New England Technology*. "Bain Bids on Huawei Mobile Handsets." September 30, 2008. *http://www.masshightech.com/stories/2008/09/29/daily17-Bain-bids-on-Huawei-mobile-handsets.html*.
- McKee, Michael, and Alex Nicholson. "Paulson Says Russia Urged China to Dump Fannie, Freddie Bonds." Bloomberg.com, January 29, 2009. *http://www.bloomberg.com/apps/news?pid=newsarchive&sid=afbSjYv3v814#*.
- McMillan, Robert. "Some SMS Networks Vulnerable to Attack." July 28, 2009. *http://tech.yahoo.com/news/pcworld/20090729/tc_pcworld/somesmsnetworksvulnerabletoattack*.
- Meredith, Robyn. Panda-ring To China? - The unwelcome sea change in U.S.-China business relations. *Forbes*, March 2, 2010. *http://www.forbes.com/2010/02/02/china-fedex-panda-diplomacy-opinions-columnists-robyn-meredith.html*.
- Meyer, David. "TeliaSonera touts first LTE '4G' launch." CNET News.com. December 14, 2009. (http://news.cnet.com/8301-1035_3-10414665-94.html)
- Miller, Sandra Kay. "Hacking at the Speed of Light." Securitysolutions.com. April 1, 2006.
- Mills, Elinor. "Researchers take control of iPhone via SMS." ZDNet.com. July 30, 2009. (http://news.zdnet.com/2100-9595_22-326501.html)
- Mills, Elinor. "SMS Messages Could Be Used to Hijack a Phone." CNet.com. April 19, 2009. *http://news.cnet.com/8301-1009_3-10222921-83.html*.
- Mobile Monday.Net. "UT Starcom Buys 3Com's Operator Assets." March 5, 2003. *http://www.lightreading.com/document.asp?doc_id=29233*.
- Moore, Malcolm. "China's Global Cyber-Espionage Network GhostNet Penetrates 103 Countries." Telegraph.co.uk. March 29, 2009. *http://www.telegraph.co.uk/news/worldnews/asia/china/5071124/Chinas-globalcyber-espionage-network-GhostNet-penetrates-103-countries.html*.
- Morrison, Wayne, and Marc Labonte."China's Holdings of U.S. Securities: Implications for the U.S. Economy." Congressional Reporting Service, CRS-7, January 9, 2008. *http://opencrs.com/document/RL34314/*.
- Mulvenon, James. "PLA Computer Network Operations: Scenarios, Doctrine, Organizations, and Capability." In *Beyond the Strait: PLA Missions Other Than Taiwan*. Edited by Roy Kamphausen, David Lai, and Andrew Scobell, Carlisle, PA: Strategic Studies Institute, April 2009. *http://www.strategicstudiesinstitute.army.mil/pdffiles/PUB910.pdf*.
- *New York Times*, "Silverlake Eyes Asia Tech Investments," November 28, 2008. *http://dealbook.blogs.nytimes.com/2008/11/25/silver-lake-eyes-asia-tech-investments/*.
- *New York Times*, "U.S. Opens Inquiry in Plan to Sell Global Crossing to Asians," April 4, 2003. *http://www.nytimes.com/2003/04/30/business/us-opens-inquiry-in-plan-to-sell-global-crossing-to-asians.html*.

- *New Zealand Herald,* "China's technological challenger," March 15, 2007. *http://www.nzherald.co.nz/telecommunications/news/article.cfm?c_id=93&objectid=10428813.*
- Newman, Bill. "Up to Bat Again – Will it be Strike Two for Huawei in the U.S.?" Inbound Acquisitions and Investments Blog, quoting *Financial Times*, April 16, 2010. *http://www.usainbounddeals.com/2010/04/articles/deals-developments/up-to-bat-again-will-it-be-strike-two-for-huawei-in-the-united-states/.*
- Ngo, Dong. "Jailbreaking iPhone could pose threat to national security, Apple claims." CNet.com. July 29, 2009. *http://reviews.cnet.com/8301-19512_7-10298646-233.html.*
- Nortel.com. "Nortel Obtains Court Orders for Creditor Protection." January 14, 2009. *http://www2.nortel.com/go/news_detail.jsp?cat_id=-8055&oid=100251347&locale=en-US.*
- Nobelprize.org. "Why Trade?" Nobelprize.org. February 28, 2006.
- Nortel.com. "Nortel, Huawei to Establish Joint Venture to Address Broadband Access Market." "Plan to Jointly Develop Ultra Broadband Products for Delivery of Converged Services." February 1, 2006. *http://www2.nortel.com/go/news_detail.jsp?cat_id=-8055&oid=100194923.*
- NPR.org. "Chinese Telecom Companies Look to Global Markets." August 16, 2005. *http://www.npr.org/templates/story/story.php?storyId=4801437.*
- Nystedt, Dan. China Mobile Wins Approval for Taiwan Subsidiary. *PCWorld*, May 11, 2010. *http://www.pcworld.com/article/196019/china_mobile_wins_approval_for_taiwan_subsidiary.html.*
- Orey, Michael. Patent Filings Surge in China. *Bloomberg Businessweek*, June 3, 2008. *http://www.businessweek.com/bwdaily/dnflash/content/jun2008/db2008063_332712.htm?chan=top+news_top+news+index_technology.*
- Pei, Minxin. The Dark Side of China's Rise. *Foreign Policy* (March/April 2006). Reprinted in Carnegie Endowment for International Peace publication. *http://www.carnegieendowment.org/publications/index.cfm?fa=view&id=18110&prog=zch.*
- Pei, Minxin. The Real Lessons from the Google-China Spat. In *The Diplomat*. Washington, DC: Carnegie Endowment for International Peace, February 3, 2010. *http://www.carnegieendowment.org/publications/index.cfm?fa=view&id=24801.*
- Peilin, Li, and Zhangyi. "Consumption Stratification In China: An Important Tool In Stirring Up Economy." Chinese Academy of Social Science (2008). *http://www.sociology.cass.cn/english/papers/P020080715377553596141.pdf.*
- Prasso, Sheridan. American made...Chinese owned: Full version. CNNMoney.com. *Fortune,* May 7, 2010. *http://money.cnn.com/2010/05/06/news/international/china_america_full.fortune.*
- Price, Ray. "Briefing to the Defense Science Board Task Force on High-Performance Microchip Supply." May 20, 2004. *http://www.acq.osd.mil/dsb/reports/ADA435563.pdf.*
- Rautu, Ovidiu. "Nokia Siemens Partners with Huawei - The agreement covers worldwide use of all standards essential patents of all parties." SoftPedia/Telecoms. September 29, 2008. *http://news.softpedia.com/news/Nokia-Siemens-Partners-With-Huawei-94374.shtm.*
- RCR Wireless. "Huawei's Aggressive Push Pays Off." September 24, 2008. *http://www.rcrwireless.com/ARTICLE/20080924/WIRELESS/809239966/huawei-146-s-aggressive-push-pays-off.*
- Reed Smith LLP. "New Amendment Rationalizes Country-of-Origin Preferences for Defense and Civilian Acquisitions." Client Bulletin 03-03, January 2003. *http://www.reedsmith.com/_db/_documents/bull0303.pdf.*

- Reuters, "Opposition Leads Bain to Call Off 3Com Deal," March 21, 2008. *http://www.nytimes.com/2008/03/21/technology/21com.html*.
- Reuters, "Russia's MTS picks Huawei for 3G Armenia Network," January 16, 2009. *http://www.reuters.com/article/idUSLG46594520090116*.
- Rogin, Josh. The top 10 Chinese cyber attacks (that we know of). *Foreign Policy* online. January 22, 2010. *http://thecable.foreignpolicy.com/posts/2010/01/22/the_top_10_chinese_cyber_attacks_that_we_know_of.*
- Schwankert, Steven. "US Congressmen Accuse China of Hacking Their Computers." Infoworld.com. IDG Network. June 12, 2008. *http://www.infoworld.com/archive/200806?page=46.*
- ScienceDaily LLC. "Stealth Attack Drains Cell Phone Batteries." August 30, 2006. *http://www.sciencedaily.com/releases/2006/08/060829090243.htm*.
- Scissors, Derek. *Chinese Foreign Investment: How Much and Where?* Business Forum China and The Heritage Foundation, August 11, 2009. *http://www.heritage.org/Research/Commentary/2009/08/Chinese-Foreign-Investment-How-Much-and-Where*.
- Scissors, Derek. "U.S.–China Strategic and Economic Dialogue: America Must Lead by Example." Washington, DC: The Heritage Foundation, May 24, 2010. *http://www.heritage.org/Research/Reports/2010/05/US-China-Strategic-and-Economic-Dialogue-America-Must-Lead-by-Example*.
- Sevastopulo, Demetri. "Hackers Breach White House System. *Financial Times*, November 6, 2008. *http://us.ft.com/ftgateway/superpage.ft?news_id=fto110620081938360726&page=2*.
- Shachtman, Noah. "Activists Launch Hack Attacks on Tehran Regime." *Wired*, June 15, 2009. *http://www.wired.com/dangerroom/2009/06/activists-launch-hack-attacks-on-tehran-regime/*.
- Shankar, Vivek, and Amy Thomson. "3Com Agrees to $2.2 Billion Takeover Offer From Bain (Update4)." Bloomberg.com, September 28, 2007. *http://www.bloomberg.com/apps/news?pid=newsarchive&sid=aC5FJiGpl5Ig&refer=us*.
- Singer, Jason, and Jason Dean. "China Mobile Nears $5.3 Billion Deal For Millicom Beijing's Biggest Purchase Overseas Would Intensify Push Into Emerging Markets." *China Daily,* May 25, 2006. *http://www.chinadaily.com.cn/world/2006-05/25/content_600127.htm*.
- Singer, Jason, and Jason Dean. "China Mobile Nears $5.3 Billion Deal For Millicom Beijing's Biggest Purchase Overseas Would Intensify Push Into Emerging Markets." *China Daily*, May 25, 2006. *http://www.chinadaily.com.cn/world/2006-05/25/content_600127.htm*.
- Smith, Michael. "Spy chiefs fear Chinese cyber attack." *Sunday Times (London)*, March 29, 2009. *http://www.timesonline.co.uk/tol/news/uk/article5993156.ece*.
- Softpedia.com. "Nokia Siemens Partners with Huawei." September 29, 2008. *http://news.softpedia.com/news/Nokia-Siemens-Partners-With-Huawei-94374.shtml*.
- Spillius, Alex. "Cyber attack 'could fell US within 15 minutes'." *Telegraph* (UK), May 7, 2010. *http://www.telegraph.co.uk/news/worldnews/northamerica/usa/7691500/Cyber-attack-could-fell-US-within-15-minutes.html*.
- Stokes, Mark A. *China's Strategic Modernization: Implications for the United States.* Carlisle, PA: Strategic Studies Institute, September 1,1999. *http://www.strategicstudiesinstitute.army.mil/pubs/display.cfm?pubID=74*.
- Strasburg, Jenny, and Rick Carew. "China Ready to Place Bets on Hedge Funds." *Wall Street Journal*, June 19, 2009. *http://online.wsj.com/article/SB124535652071428705.html*.

- Strazheim, Donald. China Buys Wall Street. Forbes.com, December 27, 2007. *http://www.forbes.com/2008/12/26/straszheim-china-cic-oped-cx_dhs_1227straszheim.html*.
- Sung, Chinmei, and Janet Ong. "Taiwan Opens 100 Industries to Chinese Investment (Update2)." Bloomberg.com. June 30, 2009. *http://www.bloomberg.com/apps/news?pid=20601080&sid=aFeN1SK55G7U*.
- Symantec Press Release. *Huawei and Symantec Commence Joint Venture*. February 5, 2008. *http://www.symantec.com/about/news/release/article.jsp?prid=20080205_01*.
- Szor, Peter. *The Art of Computer Virus Research and Defense*. Boston, MA: Addison-Wesley, 2005, pp. 474–481.
- TechTarget. "SMiShing." SearchMobileComputing.com. Definitions. January 30, 2007. *http://searchmobilecomputing.techtarget.com/sDefinition/0,,sid40_gci1241308,00.html*.
- TelecomsEurope.net. "Cisco, Juniper Lose Routing Market Share in 2009." "Cisco and Juniper's combined market share fell from 69% in 2008 to 59% in 2009. Huawei and Alcatel-Lucent gained much of the share these companies lost." February 22, 2010. *http://www.telecomseurope.net/content/cisco-juniper-lose-routing-market-share-2009.*
- TeleGeography's ComsUpdate. "Guine Telecom to receive USD50m in Chinese investment." October 21, 2008. *http://www.telegeography.com/cu/article.php?article_id=25675*.
- Texas Instruments Press Release. "TI Completes Sale of Sensor Control Business to Bain Capital." April 26, 2006. *http://focus.ti.com/pr/docs/preldetail.tsp?sectionId=594&prelId=c06022*.
- Thomas, Timothy L. "Taiwan Examines Chinese Information Warfare." *High Frontiers* Vol. 5, No. 3 (May 2009). *http://www.afspc.af.mil/shared/media/document/AFD-090519-102.pdf*.
- Thomson Financial News, "China Unicom acquires Netcom," June 2, 2008.
- Thomson Reuters, "2008 Global Innovation Study," March 24, 2009. *http://science.thomsonreuters.com/press/2009/innovation_study/*.
- Thornburgh, Nathan. The Invasion of the Chinese Cyberspies (And the Man Who Tried to Stop Them). *Time*, August 29, 2005. *http://www.time.com/time/magazine/article/0,9171,1098961,00.html.*
- Timmons, Heather. "India Tells Mobile Firms to Delay Deals for Chinese Telecom Equipment," *New York Times*, April 30, 2010. *http://www.nytimes.com/2010/05/01/business/global/01delhi.html*.
- Timmons, Heather. "India Tells Mobile Firms to Delay Deals for Chinese Telecom Equipment." *New York Times*, April 30, 2010. *http://www.nytimes.com/2010/05/01/business/global/01delhi.html*.
- U.S. Department of Defense. *Defense Science Board Task Force on High-Performance Microchip Supply*. Arlington, VA: Office of the Under Secretary of Defense for Acquisition, Technology, and Logistics, February 2005. *http://www.acq.osd.mil/dsb/reports/ADA435563.pdf*.
- U.S.-China Economic and Security Review Commission. Various Annual Reports to Congress. *http://www.uscc.gov*.
- Ventre, Daniel. "China's Strategy for Information Warfare: A Focus on Energy." *Journal of Energy Security* (May 18, 2010). *http://www.ensec.org/index.php?option=com_content&view=article&id=241:critical-energy-infrastructure-security-and-chinese-cyber-threats&catid=106:energysecuritycontent0510&Itemid=361*.
- Ventre, Daniel. China's Strategy for Information Warfare: A Focus on Energy." *Journal of Energy Security* (May 18, 2010). *http://www.ensec.org/index.php?option=com_content&view=article&id=241:critical-*

energy-infrastructure-security-and-chinese-cyber-
threats&catid=106:energysecuritycontent0510&Itemid=361.
- Voice&Data Online. "ZTE Right Pricing." September 3, 2008.
  http://voicendata.ciol.com/content/service_provider/108090303.asp.
- *Wall Street Journal,* "China's Huawei May Sell a Stake Abroad," May 8, 2008.
- *Wall Street Journal,* "China's Telecom Gear Makers, Once Laggards at Home, Pass
  Foreign Rivals, ' April 10, 2010.
  *http://wwwen.zte.com.cn/en/press_center/press_clipping/200904/t20090410_171143.ht
  ml*.
- *Wall Street Journal,* "Chinese Barriers to Foreign Firms – Good for Innovation," April
  15,2010. *http://blogs.wsj.com/digits/2010/04/15/chinese-barriers-to-foreign-firms-good-
  for-innovation/*.
- Walt, Stephen, M. "Is the cyber threat overblown?" *Foreign Policy* online. March 30,
  2010.
  *http://walt.foreignpolicy.com/posts/2010/03/30/is_the_cyber_threat_overblown?obref=ob
  network*.
- War impact maps of the Serbian networks during their 1999 conflict. Available at
  http://www.cheswick.com/ches/map/yu/index.html.
- Washington State. Office of the Attorney General. "Cell Phones Under Attack: How to
  block text spam and viruses." December 19, 2007.
  (*http://www.sciencedaily.com/releases/2006/08/060829090243.htm*.
- Weisman, Steven R. "Sale of 3Com to Huawei is derailed by U.S. security concerns."
  New York Times, February 21, 2008.
  *http://www.nytimes.com/2008/02/21/business/worldbusiness/21iht-
  3com.1.10258216.html*.
- Whelan, Carolyn. China's New Frontier. *Fortune*, June 25, 2009. CNNMoney.com.
  *http://money.cnn.com/2009/06/23/technology/china_telecom_latin_america.fortune/index
  .htm*.
- Wilson, Richard. "China Goes for 4G LTE in a Big Way." Electronicsweekly.com. July 29,
  2009. *http://www.electronicsweekly.com/Articles/2009/07/29/46620/china-goes-for-4g-
  lte-in-a-big-way.htm*.
- WiMAX (Worldwide Interoperability for Microwave Access). "What is WiMAX."
  WiMAX.com. *http://www.wimax.com/education.*
- *XChange.* Huawei: 'It' Vendor 2010. January 8, 2010.
  http://www.von.com/articles/2010/01/huawei-it-vendor-of-2010.aspx.
- Xiaobei, Cheng. "How to Stimulate Domestic Consumption?" *China Today*, February 25,
  2009. *http://www.chinatoday.com.cn/ctenglish/se/txt/2009-02/25/content_180244.htm*.
- Xiaohong , Ouyang. "China's Sovereign Wealth Fund Favors Real Economy." *Economic
  Observer*, March 2, 2009.
  http://www.eeo.com.cn/ens/finance_investment/2009/03/06/131432.shtml.
- Yeo, Vivian. "Chinese Firms Behind 'Sexy Space' Trojan." CNet.com. July 22, 2009.
  http://news.cnet.com/8301-1009_3-10292917-83.html.
- Zachary, G. Pascal. *See No Evil - How American businesses collaborate with China's
  repressive government.*ThirdWorldTraveler.com. November 2005.
  http://www.thirdworldtraveler.com/Transnational_corps/See_No_Evil_China.html.

Additional information derived from selected studies, papers, transcripts, lectures, conversations, and collaborations with sources, public and private:

The University of Oxford, Stanford University, Harvard University, Reperi Analysis Center, Trends Digest, RAND Corporation, Carnegie Endowment for International Peace, U.S. Department of Commerce's National Telecommunications and Information Administration, U.S. Federal Communications Commission, National Telecommunications Cooperative Association, U.S. National Institute of Standards and Technology, U.S. National Defense University, U.S. Department of Energy Idaho National Laboratory, U.S. Federal Bureau of Investigation, U.S. Department of Homeland Security, U.S. Department of State, U.S. Air Force Space Command, U.S. National Science Foundation, U.S. Department of Commerce National Technical Information Service, U.S. Department of the Army Foreign Military Studies Office, U.S. Library of Congress, Asia Programme at the Royal United Services Institute for Defence Studies in Whitehall London, Technische Universität Berlin, The Heritage Foundation, Council on Foreign Relations, Foreign Policy Research Institute, APICS Association for Operations Management, European Organization for Nuclear Research, MITRE Corporation, Jawaharlal Nehru University, Institute for Defence Studies and Analyses in New Delhi, Regional Center for Strategic Studies in Sri Lanka, and various other private corporations, universities, individuals, and government institutions.

Other useful publicly available information sources:

The Republic of China Government Information Office (Taiwan), Fudan University, Zhejiang University, Shanghai Academy of Social Sciences, Lanzhou University, Shanghai Center for International Studies, Ministry of Foreign Affairs of the People's Republic of China, China Investment Corporation, China Academy of Military Science, and various other Republic of China (Taiwan) and People's Republic of China sources of publications available as English translations through the U.S. Department of Commerce's National Technical Information Service or other open source translations.

Special thanks to those individuals, including business executives and outside subject-matter experts, who volunteered time, thoughtfulness, and energies to contribute to this report.

www.ingramcontent.com/pod-product-compliance
Lightning Source LLC
Chambersburg PA
CBHW080104010626

45794CB00014B/3111